START OVER TO WIN

HOW TO BUILD THE **LIFE YOU WANT** WHEN YOU DON'T HAVE EVERYTHING YOU NEED

MAX KONAN

Start Over to Win:
How to Build the Life You Want When You Don't Have Everything You Need

Written by Max Konan

Design and cover art by Peaceful Profits.

Paperback ISBN: 978-1-967587-59-9
eBook ISBN: 978-1-967587-60-5

This book is a work of nonfiction. It represents the accuracy of the events mentioned to the best of the author's recollection. Some names in the book have been replaced to maintain the privacy of certain individuals.

The information contained in this book is provided for educational purposes only and should not be construed as legal, financial, tax, or investment advice. Readers are strongly encouraged to consult with a qualified and licensed professional who can provide advice tailored to their individual circumstances. Laws, regulations, and financial practices vary across countries, states, and regions. Market conditions, returns, and outcomes will differ over time and cannot be guaranteed. While every effort has been made to provide accurate and timely information at the time of writing, we make no representations or warranties regarding completeness, accuracy, or applicability. We are not making any official legal or financial recommendations. The examples, figures, and principles presented herein are for illustrative and educational purposes only. Any decisions you make are solely your responsibility.

This book is dedicated to my strong and loving mother,
K. Adjoua Ponou.

TABLE OF CONTENTS

INTRODUCTION

Have you ever imagined impossible dreams, knowing that even though they seemed unlikely, everything in you wanted to make those dreams into your reality somehow? You aren't alone. Maybe your journey has been full of starts and stops, just like mine. Or it could be that what you wanted to do looked simpler in theory than it felt when you took action. I've been there.

When I was a young man, growing up in Côte d'Ivoire (formerly called the Ivory Coast) in Africa, I used to stand on a bridge that stood between where I lived and where my school was and look at the different company men and politicians who would pass by. These men had Black skin like me. And they were being pulled and pushed by our own culture and the influence of the French—also like me. However, they were wealthy enough to own fancy cars that they weren't even required to drive themselves, having drivers who chauffeured them around.

I knew that someday, I wanted to be one of those company men or political leaders, even though that seemed so far outside of my reach. Yes, I desired to be successful enough to be driven in a fancy car, but more importantly, I wanted to have enough physical, mental, and professional resources—like what I saw the wealthy men have—to be able to bounce back from any obstacle life put in front of me.

You see, scarcity in general was a character in my life—a physical presence I could feel. And when I say scarcity, I mean that you lack the resources you need.

There was emotional scarcity, resource scarcity, and mindset scarcity in the world all around me. As we take this journey together, you will learn about these three types of scarcity, and one more—the scarcity of grief.

As you step into my story, you will see that I was able to hit the reset button on all of the scarcity in my life numerous times, no matter what challenge or obstacle stood in my way. And, I was able to eventually realize the dream I had as a young man standing on that bridge wishing to become a man of importance.

I have made it my mission to prove to you, as you read your way through these pages, that by using the methods and techniques I will share here, you too can always hit the reset button when it comes to the challenges you face in your own life.

No matter what happens in your life, if you keep dreaming and looking for alternative ways through obstacles whenever you reach a setback, you will be able to leverage scarcity and adversity to build your own life full of meaning, just like I did. And you'll do so based on serving others in a way that supports you and your family while also making the world a better place—through your ability to create a clear vision, make strategic choices, and determine your willingness to start over again and again, as many times as it takes, to win.

If you can learn how to dream big while remaining flexible—so that you can pivot when difficult things happen in your life—you will have the chance to accomplish your own dreams.

At the same time, I know that life rarely happens in a straight line—mine certainly hasn't.

What I don't want to do in this book is show you a linear path from where I stood dreaming on that bridge to becoming the CEO of a successful company that is making the world a better place. Real life rarely happens that way. Instead, I want to show you that in spite of having to push the reset button on my life several times, I was able to use my lack of resources in each situation to realize which thoughts, tools, and relationships I needed to move forward. It was actually because of the very real presence of scarcity that I knew how to approach every goal I've pursued in life. And you too can learn to leverage scarcity in the same way to keep building momentum as you step closer to your dreams.

Against all odds—I went from being in a horrible accident as a young boy (one that shattered my knowledge of how to walk and my ability to understand which side of my body was right or left), to moving into a city that was full of different kinds of danger, to leaving my family to go to middle school, to losing my mother, to becoming an expat in the United States and losing everything I had built there while having to start again several times. Through each of these events, I learned to take the negative idea of scarcity (not having enough resources) and leverage it to build the life I've always wished for.

As this journey unfolded, I was able to pivot and adapt constantly and with consistency. I worked several jobs in different industries. I moved to the United States and worked with boys who had special needs in a group home. I went back to school and learned how to be a teacher who focused on special education. And eventually, I was able to found a business, A Bright Future, Inc., that does the good work (as I call it) of helping adults with limitations live in a way that allows them to be part of their communities while living independently.

My heart now prompts me to share with you the most important, life-changing lessons I learned from having to start over again and again without ever letting my impossible dreams die. And how, in spite of what I have faced, I was able to take the negative idea of scarcity (not having enough resources) and leverage it to build a life that gave me deep satisfaction.

This ability to know how to leverage scarcity so that you can create the life you desire is what I want to give you.

I'm not going to tell you that the journey from where you are to making your life into one that you've always wanted will be easy. It won't. But, as you'll see in my story, it's possible.

Especially if you're willing to start over again as each new phase of your life unfolds.

My Dream Versus My Reality

My reality didn't look anything like the dreams I had for my future—for so many different reasons. Even though I had navigated many challenges as a boy and a young man, another huge shift happened when my mother's ongoing health issues caused a sudden decline.

For as long as I can remember, my mother had always battled some illness. As an adult, just as I was looking forward to going off to graduate school so I could start living my life, she came to need more consistent support.

As soon as I heard, I began to imagine what it would be like to delay all of my plans so that I could go and take care of her. To support my mother and love her in the most practical way. Out of all my siblings and half-siblings, I knew I was the one she needed because of the bond we had created when I was recovering from my accident all those years before.

But before I could make a single change in any of my plans, the unthinkable happened: My mother passed away. The woman who had loved and supported me through every major change and challenge, my rock and champion. The person who felt like she was my entire life. The one who had nursed me back to health after my own medical struggles due to the accident that happened when I was just 4 years old.

When I lost her, in that moment, I realized that what I wanted—more than anything else in this world—was to take care of others. Those who were struggling like my mother. Those who understood the same difficulties I went through after my accident.

A little while after her death, I experienced the profound privilege of becoming a parent. And when I looked at my son, all of those feelings in me, the desire to be a caretaker, grew even stronger. The same thing happened when my daughter was born.

What I didn't realize back then was that the success I had dreamed about all those years ago—standing on that bridge— would eventually come true. Not because of how smart I was or how many plans I made but because of how much that feeling of wanting to care for others came to dominate my life in a good way. And because I was willing to start over again and learn something new about myself and the world each time I was met with a new challenge rooted in scarcity.

As I mentioned, one of the paths I had to start over was when I was still new in the United States. This led me to work inside of a group home where I met Paul. He's someone you will read about later in the book, but the quick version of the story is this: Paul was alone. And he hadn't chosen to be alone like I had. It was my choice to move from the Ivory Coast to the United States in the hope of discovering more opportunities, knowing I didn't have a good support system or community to interact with.

On the other hand, seeing Paul experience what I would call forced loneliness completely changed my life. Not one choice he had made caused him to be alone, but still, there was no one in his life who wanted to support or take care of him. This truth was shocking to me because in Africa, we would take care of those around us by bringing them into our families when needed. As I looked at that situation through my own cultural lens, I kept coming back to the fact that it had been my choice to leave and encounter the loneliness I experienced as an expatriate in the US. Paul's loneliness was forced upon him by the people who had abandoned him.

It is because of children like Paul and the special needs students I worked with that I was inspired to found A Bright Future, Inc. Our collective mission is to help special needs adults become active members of their communities, no matter what limitations they face.

As I think about boys like Paul and students with special needs and the unique struggles they face because of scarcity, I feel even more inspired to take on this project and write this book to help you.

Because scarcity doesn't have to mean that all of your dreams die.

Who Is This Book for?

When I sat down to work on this project, I was thinking about your future, my dear reader. There are so many young people I've interacted with who were talented and amazing, but they didn't have the guidance they needed to understand that even in the middle of intense scarcity—in all of its different forms— scarcity itself could be used to help build out their dreams.

That is why I wanted to write this book, to help you as the world of the future and its possibilities lie before you and to teach you to navigate through scarcity, using it as a tool to move forward instead of fearing what it can do to your unique future.

As I thought about what I wanted to say in this project, there were hundreds of faces that popped into my head—all of the young people I've worked with over the years. One of the things that I'm most proud of is being a father. I love my children without condition. It is my pleasure to cheer them on as they work through struggles they face in their own lives. But as a father, I also recognize that not everyone has a parent or a mentor to do the same thing I want to do for my kids: to help them see just how beautiful and fulfilling this life can be. There are many different reasons why you might not have the support you should. Maybe your parents have a different perspective than you. Maybe you lost one of your parents when you were young, like I did.

Whatever situation you are in right now, I want you to know that whether you're facing personal uncertainty or professional unpredictability due to some kind of scarcity, this book was created with my entire heart to support you. To encourage you. And to remind you that even when things seem or feel impossible, you can still create a clear path forward.

But What If Your Dreams Don't Come True?

Well, dear reader, let's start this journey together with a confession from me. I did not always believe that I would be able to live the dreams I had as a young man on that bridge between where I lived and where I went to school. But one day, I realized something that helped me hold my aspirations with an open hand.

When you dream, you are the only one who knows about those dreams. And if you don't manage to accomplish them, that's okay. No one is going to get frustrated or mad at you because you didn't make those dreams into reality—they live in the privacy of your mind.

This was such a freeing concept for me that it gave me room to be flexible—along with the ability to start again, pivoting as I went along on my personal path. And I want that same freedom for you.

Once you are released from the pressure of making your dreams come true in a specific way or within a certain time period, you will begin to see how you can leverage scarcity to navigate any of the struggles life brings. You can start over again, overcome any obstacles that come your way, and use the fact that you might be missing resources or need an adjusted mindset to discover a path forward to your dreams. All within the privacy of your mind.

What Can You Expect From This Book?

The best way I know to help you is to use a tool that creates important learning opportunities in my culture: circle time. As young people in villages of the Côte d'Ivoire experience, there are moments during the week when entire families gather to learn. The older relatives will tell family stories that teach the young people how they can avoid certain mistakes, embrace life-building triumphs, and overcome terrible fears.

That is what I want to do with you inside these pages—to form our very own circle time. But instead of me telling you the stories with my spoken voice, I'm going to write them down in words (unless you're listening to the audiobook).

Each chapter will have a story from my life that I will use to illustrate a principle to help you understand how to leverage scarcity by starting again to move forward. Then, I'll break down the meaning of the concepts from each story. Finally, in each chapter, you'll see a section called "Reset, Restart, Repeat," where you will have the opportunity to think through how the story and the concepts I've shared can be applied to your own life.

In part 1, we will focus on what it looks like to lose something and be able to start again. This has been a huge part of my story, and I imagine that if you're reading this book, you can relate.

In part 2, we will take a look at how the concept of starting again can create anxiety and how allowing the idea of pivoting to become your friend can help you react to that anxiety. To start again brings all sorts of new chances to build a life that will support your dreams.

Finally, in part 3, the main focus will be on how feelings of hope, moments of transition, and sparks of victory can contribute to huge wins in your life if you are willing to start again.

Are you ready to go on a new journey? To start again with me as your guide and supporter as you work to make your impossible-seeming dreams into reality? I promise that the time it takes to read through this book—and complete the exercises in order to carve out your own path—will be worth every second.

With a heart full of gratitude and service,
Max Konan

PART 1

SEE IT, LOSE IT, & START AGAIN

CHAPTER 1

Nothing But an Amen

Earlier, I shared that I experienced a significant accident when I was 4 years old. When I heard my family members talk about me before that traumatic event and after, it sounded like they were describing two totally different people. And that separation between the before, the after, and the changes that happened along the way exists not just in me—but in everyone.

The idea of before and after, and how that separation changed my life, was a concept that would become consistent in my story as I faced each new moment of needing to start again.

Hold onto that idea for a moment.

In this chapter, I don't want to talk about the accident just yet. I want to talk about the before times, when I was just a tiny boy. Back before my world changed in the first cataclysmic way— who I was before I experienced my first major reset.

Even though I was only 4 years old, I started to realize how internal and external opportunities had already begun to shape who I would become. As we journey through these next pages, I am going to show you when an opportunity in my life was internal or external. And I invite you to look at your own story through the same lens.

External opportunities come from the world around you; in other words, they are already created and established before you encounter them. This could take the form of education, career possibilities, friends and the influence they have on you, or even how outside places and cultures teach you new things.

Internal opportunities, however, come from inside of you. They are made of your thoughts, your family relationships, and the boundaries you learn inside of your family.

Before we go through my story, though, I want to make a request—with an open and sensitive heart.

Consider Me

Part of me wants to hold the setting of my story close, fold it into the beats of my heart, and not share it with you. How many times have you heard or read about poverty in Africa? This time, though, as you approach the parts of my life I want to entrust to you, I humbly ask that you become curious about what new things my story can show you.

What I came to realize in the process of planning this book is that my life isn't a stereotype just because scarcity touched my circumstances at such a young age. It's also not a stereotype because I experienced a traumatic accident that could have happened to anyone, anywhere in the world.

I recognize now how my background weaves together the beautiful tapestry of who I am. Where I grew up and when events happened will give you the context that you need to see how scarcity was a tangible force in my life—from day one.

At the same time, as you'll see, I also experienced a traumatic brain injury (TBI) at a young age. This has affected everything in my life, but in regards to this book, you need to know that I might speak and write differently than you would expect. When I started this project, I attempted to change my communication so it would be as easy to understand as possible, but that also stripped most of my voice from the writing. In the end, I didn't want that because I can't properly tell the story of my life if it means removing myself.

If there are moments when you have to read a sentence more than once, please be patient with me. I hope that at the end of this book, you will think the message was worth your effort— just like it would be with a sophisticated piece of literature.

So, as you read on, I ask you to be gentle (and reserve your judgement) as you think about my TBI, my home, my family, and my culture, dear reader. Instead of being critical, I ask you to engage your curiosity about how my unique geographic location and circumstances have contributed to who I am today.

Not Quite the Middle—How Scarcity Entered My Life

Growing up in Côte d'Ivoire, in West Africa—surrounded by Liberia, Guinea, Burkina Faso, Mali, and Ghana—there were certain unspoken truths that we all understood. There were different types of living. There were villages for farmers, the slums with shanty houses going up and down overnight just outside of the cities, developed houses formed into neighborhoods made for those with low income called social homes, the middle neighborhoods with standard homes for blue-collar workers, and giant houses on more expansive lots of land for the rich.

In the villages where farmers lived, there would be no electricity. People would get their water from public wells, and often, they didn't even have candles to light their way in the dark hours after sunset.

Before I was born, my family was able to move from our village into one of the social homes in the city of Abidjan because my father had a job as a human resources manager. His career was an external opportunity he paid attention to and leveraged to get us into our new home.

When our family lived in the village, there would be circle time to share wisdom with each other in the form of oral narratives. This practice was so popular that when I was growing up, an elder (someone's grandfather) would come on the TV at 5:00 p.m. each day to host a region-wide circle-time program.

Although my maternal grandmother was alive, I didn't meet her until I was an adult—which meant she couldn't be my circle-time leader. I also didn't have any other grandparents left who lived nearby to give my siblings and me circle time. And the grandfather on the TV didn't really feel like a family member, so his advice just didn't impact me in the same way.

Plus, my family's change from village life to living in social housing meant no outdoor space for a fire. Those things meant no more circle time for our family, which was devastating to me. You see, circle time was where children could safely learn any lessons they needed to know about life. I am told my brothers and sisters enjoyed circle time consistently in our old family home in the village. Culturally, the shift away from villages also meant that there was a lot of social pressure for us to embrace a more modern life, which did not include circle time. At least, this is why I believe families in the social homes abandoned the practice.

But with that learning opportunity gone from our modern home before I was born, I had to observe directly what got my siblings and half-siblings into trouble if I wanted to avoid getting punished myself. (Having both siblings and half-siblings was normal in my culture, and we learned to distinguish the difference at a young age.) Edith, my sister, was my best friend in addition to being my sister, and she taught me a lot. I'm sure you can imagine, though, that observation alone didn't feel like such a safe way to learn. As I grew older, I noticed that our family's move didn't just change our traditions—it changed my father's priorities as he worked to embrace the new social status our shift in housing created.

The home he purchased was modest, with three bedrooms for 12 of us (the number seemed to constantly change as people moved in and out), including my parents, siblings, and half-siblings. I remember my father building, renovating, and adding to our home. Over time, he turned our three-bedroom, one-bathroom house into a five-bedroom, two-bathroom house with an outhouse in the back.

Part of the reason the number of residents in our house changed so frequently was that the people who worked for my mother as part of her trading business would often sleep on our living room floor.

It was important to my father that his house was considered fancy and modern because of the status he now felt compelled to embrace and display, so he worked to make the house fit his ideals. We had nice tiles and a water faucet. We also had both a Western-style kitchen and an African kitchen with an open fire.

At some point, though, there was a financial crisis, and my father's job went away. Scarcity became my reality from that point on—and scarcity shaped most of what I remember about my childhood.

The external opportunity my father had been given to get us into a social home had changed our situation, but scarcity changed it further. That's when the fight to have enough began in my life.

The lifestyle that my siblings had lived before my father lost his job is unknown to me. What I do remember is the sticky, hot social home in the rain season. The drops of water came so hard and fast that the walls would fill with them, and water would spill out onto the floor. Then, our tubs, toilets, and sinks would back up and overflow.

Even in difficult moments, though, my house was also full of love. If we wanted to have a party, we didn't need to invite anyone over because of how many of us there already were. I don't remember getting presents for birthdays or holidays, but I remember the rooms of my house often being filled with laughter. These family relationships were the biggest and most important internal opportunities I was given as a child. Sure, sometimes there was yelling and crying, but that wasn't something I had the power to change.

We grew up speaking our mother tongue, Baoulé. But at school, we learned French. For my siblings, there was a constant push and pull between our African heritage and the Western world. This cultural standoff between my older siblings and my parents created tension that I felt even before I started school myself. I was so excited for whatever was going to come next—and in a lot of ways that translated into me being impatient. Because of that, my passion for life, even then, was big. So big. And with my passion and energy came consequences—as you'll soon see.

Life as Someone Bundi

The word *bundi* means that you run everywhere all the time. I remember hearing my family members use that word to describe me often. I was naturally curious and outgoing and was never short on energy—the kind that allowed me to bound and then rebound after a brief period of being tired.

My being bundi wasn't always easy for my parents to deal with. They both worked and had lots of kids to take care of. And my *passion pour la vie* (passion for life) surpassed anything they had dealt with before.

When I think about how to describe how bundi I was, one story strongly comes to mind. As part of our culture, there was a man who would go around, making the swish noise with his circumcision scissors, and if he passed by your house, you were safe. But if he came into your house, you had better watch out—it was time for *your* circumcision to take place. This meant your parents had scrounged and saved because the services of this man were costly. I can remember the sound of his scissors in my mind even now.

One day, I saw this man with the scissors and thought, *He has come for me.* So, I did what any logical bundi boy would do: I ran away and climbed up into a tree.

My brothers had to go up into the tree in order to yank me down. *That* is how bundi I was. My energy allowed me to show up in big ways to play with and entertain my siblings, but it also allowed me to run and hide. It gave me the strength to *resist*.

Looking back, I wonder how long my parents had to save to pay the circumcision man to perform my circumcision—with his ever-swishing scissors.

Praying and Hoping for More

From what I remember, religion was always part of my life. We had the influence of Western Christianity, but we also had our African practices and sacrifices. There were ancestors we were meant to worship and rituals to follow. But we also had a white baby Jesus to pray to, which was interesting because we were Black. Everything was mixed together like a well-seasoned stew. My parents taught me the concept of God, and it was that God who I would pray to when I desperately needed a physical *something*. Because of how many of us there were, there seemed to be an ongoing list of important items to pray for.

With the sheer number of people in my childhood home, even things that might seem as simple as having enough food for everyone proved to be a challenge.

My mother was a strong business woman, but she also had health issues. I remember hearing that she wasn't supposed to have as many kids as she did, but I never really understood if there was a certain health condition she experienced.

She had stomach problems that would come and go. Then there was her blood pressure. I don't know if it was too high or too low. There were births when she had a C-section, and some of the babies wouldn't make it through the surgery.

I share all that to say that my mom wasn't always able to work. And after my father lost his job, her income was all we had. This created more need. More scarcity. My mom's business was an external opportunity she had, but she wasn't always able to use it due to her health issues.

When my brothers and sisters started school, they needed uniforms. At that time, in Côte d'Ivoire, if you didn't have a uniform, you couldn't go to school. And missing out on the opportunity to go to school meant you would never have the tools to change your situation.

Without consistent money for uniforms, my brothers and sisters worked to make theirs last two, three, or four years— hoping that the holes they had repaired wouldn't burst open and expose the skin underneath. I knew that someday it would be my turn and that I would need to pray to that Christian God that our family could afford a uniform for me.

At the same time, we had a small black-and-white television, purchased by my dad, and a record player that had been given to us by my uncle. These bringers of information helped me envision a different way of life. Worlds where abundance wasn't an impossible dream—it was reality.

The Pull Between Cultures

I also felt the tension between our African heritage and the French way of living. You see, Côte d'Ivoire had been colonized by France in the past, which was what caused there to be so many Western influences. Even in our African schools, in the younger grades, my siblings spent half of their lessons sitting in front of a television, watching children's educational programming in French. Those French cultural influences then spilled into how my siblings acted at home, which prompted a lot of fights between my older brothers and sisters and my parents, as my siblings were at an age when they were exploring their own ideas and identities and those new thoughts seemed at odds with the traditions of my parents.

I could also see the way that the French and African beliefs and approaches impacted the ideas, fashion influences, and religious beliefs inside my family. My brothers and sisters started to dress in clothes that were made with African fabric but cut into French styles.

The vinyl records my siblings brought home and listened to changed from African melodies and beats to songs in French that spoke about concepts we wouldn't have otherwise been able to imagine.

All of this contributed to the truths from different corners of the world that lived simultaneously in my young mind:

- In African culture, you should always respect your elders. This meant you could not correct someone older than you, even if they were wrong. In Western thinking, one needed to be efficient to correct others, meaning quick and with clear, measurable outcomes.

- At home, in African culture, when we spoke to our parents, we couldn't look them in the eye because that was a sign of disrespect. I didn't even know what the eyes of my parents looked like until I saw them in pictures much later in life. In contrast, from the perspective of Western thinking, you should be independent, look others directly in the eyes, and make your own decisions for your life.

- In African culture, you would always have to agree with someone when you were in their presence. In Western culture, it was good to ask questions and challenge the thinking of others.

- You always eat and do everything with your right hand in African culture, or you get beaten. (This is important to note in my particular situation for reasons I'll explain in the next chapter, where you will understand how this fact shaped my story.) Western culture uses both hands for many things. Left-handed people are not considered taboo.

- In African culture, you would use locally produced food because it was affordable, and everyone knew how to cook it. In the Western world, they used some exported groceries, meaning that European food was expensive. And even though you might want it, your parents didn't know how to make it, so you would stick to African food.

Even though there was a push and pull of cultural truths in my mind, it was in the Western way of my thinking that I realized I could dream of a different life. This was an important external opportunity for me because, in this specific case, without traveling, I still had an opportunity to learn about another culture.

Even in my 4-year-old heart, this push and pull of cultures acted like a spark that sunk in and formed roots. I knew that I wanted to be someone important someday. That I wanted to work in a city where the important people had jobs. That I would make sure my family could afford uniforms, food, and essentials without so much stress and prayer required.

As an adult, I look back at this before time and realize that even then, I had started to shape the way I felt about myself. I was strong, curious, and outspoken—bundi. I had goals and plans for my life, even at such a young age. But all of that was about to change. And that change would come because I wasn't content just to sit at home. I wanted to live my life.

Back then, what I didn't know was that the next phase of my life, although extremely limited and difficult, would bring me certain gifts that I would celebrate in the scarcity-filled years that were ahead of me.

As a child, I knew only uncertainty. There were too many mouths to feed and bodies to clothe. I didn't yet understand how to leverage scarcity by looking at the opportunities around me. Now, as an adult, I can look and see which external opportunities—the ones I couldn't create or control—there were. I can also look at which internal opportunities existed to guide and help me.

Let's look at both of these concepts more closely so you can see which opportunities you have had and currently have in your own life.

External and Internal Opportunities

As you know by now, one of the biggest obstacles I faced was scarcity—not having enough. As I look back on that earlier time for me and my family, I realize now that there were two specific categories of opportunities that we experienced. I want to explore what these two categories mean as you begin to learn how to leverage scarcity in your own life. Let's take a look.

In your everyday life, there are two opportunities that shape the way you live: external and internal.

External Opportunities

These influences come from anything outside of you. This was something I noticed even when I was young. When you are looking at an external opportunity, you have no influence or control over it. It's not part of your immediate environment, like your home. These are opportunities that you can't sit down and create. They come completely from the outside. Like when my father lost his job.

One external opportunity is education. It's external because it was developed by someone else. For example, let's say you're in university. Maybe there are educational standards that determine what you need to be learning at age 18 as a college freshman, specific courses that you have no control over. But then, you have different learning objectives and more freedom when you become a sophomore who has completed the core requirements. The university has created this entire system with you in mind to help you, and you can take advantage of that.

The way I look at external opportunities today is with gratitude. I want to take each of these moments seriously because someone else had to put in the work to create and test a plan that would help others (including me).

I knew that if I took what others were teaching me seriously, then I could learn the elements and information they were sharing. And that this knowledge would help me gain wisdom and understanding. These were things I needed so I could get a good job.

As I grew and continued to observe what was going on around me, I came up with four external opportunities that I could use to build the life I wanted:

- Education
- Career
- Friends
- Change of environment/trips

Let's take a brief look at how each of these external opportunities can shape the way we interact with the world for the better.

Education

We already explored this concept in the example I gave you when looking at the way university years might be structured, but I want to emphasize that anytime someone else has done the work for you, it is worth evaluating how that work can benefit you so that you are not forced to start from nothing.

Career

When you're first starting out, it can feel like you don't have any of the skills you need to get the position you want. But life is full of external opportunities that you've been through—ones that have trained you to interact with others in a professional way. Once you're established in your career, that's when you can look at what you need to do next in order to get a promotion and raise.

The path is already there, but you have to be willing to ask which way to go on that path so that you can adjust accordingly. The reason a career is external is that it is outside of you. The main opportunity in a career is financial, but don't overlook the experience and related opportunities your career can have for you in addition to money.

Friends

Having smart, kind, and generous friends is one of the most important external opportunities possible. Friends have the potential to influence you, cheer you on, teach you things you don't already know, and build you up. This is why it is important to be deliberate about the friends you spend time with. If you want to know whether a friend is someone who can help you and that you would love to help in return, ask yourself this question: *When we spend time together, am I being recharged or drained?* You'll want to spend more time with those who recharge you because no one enjoys feeling drained.

A valuable friendship is also one where care goes both ways, so it is also worth noting whether or not you know how to ask friends for help. If not, it's time to start practicing. And when they ask you for help and you're able to say yes, do it! This will not only help you build a stronger relationship with them, but it will also give you opportunities to grow and change as you work to make their life better.

Change of Environment/Trips

Stepping out of your comfort zone will give your mind the freedom to approach problems and solutions in a different way than you would at home, inside your commonplace environment. Many of the most important lessons I've learned have taken place when I was willing to move to a different part of the country or change continents altogether. When you are in your house, you are in a cocoon made of what is familiar to you. But when you adventure out into the world, you gain a new perspective. This eventually happened to me through my experience with French culture once I started school, and before that, I felt moments of this by watching how my siblings adjusted their behavior.

While moving creates a deeper and more freeing experience, taking a trip can replicate that on a mini level. One extremely helpful thing about this kind of external opportunity is that trips give us opportunities to gain new perspectives about whatever problems we're facing. It could be that when you start a trip, something going on in your life feels heavy and impossible to deal with. As you travel, things that seemed serious often become less threatening. Now, let's take a look at the next kind of chance you have for growth.

Internal Opportunities

These are the moments of hope that happen at home, in your mind, and through the relationships you have with your family members. I have found four different types of internal opportunities that can help you realize your place in the world as you learn and grow:

- Family relationships
- Boundaries set by parents
- Meditation
- Reflection

In my story, you saw that even at an early age, the way I interacted with my parents and my family shaped who I would eventually become. This is how internal opportunities work.

In the next chapter, you'll see how the accident I survived influenced several of these internal concepts. For now, I want to take you through the basics of each one.

Family Relationships

When you are at home, you have the opportunity to learn by watching the people around you and being curious about their actions and behaviors. For me, I would ask myself questions like, *Well, when my brother got in trouble, what was he doing? And how can I avoid getting punished by avoiding those actions?* I am thankful I wasn't an only child. You can also look at how your parents interact with their friends. What behaviors are considered positive, and which ones are looked at as negative? By observing the interactions of those around you, it is possible to notice how things play out over time—the preferences people have, the cultural expectations that exist for you and others around you, and which actions result in discipline and which result in praise. This practice of being observant can teach you a lot.

Maybe at this point in the book, you're looking back and thinking, *What lessons did I learn from my own family relationships?* This is a wonderful question to ask because of how intensely those relationships shape who you are—for better or for worse. The truth is that even negative interactions have lessons built into them that we can use as opportunities to grow.

Boundaries Set by Parents

When we are growing up, our parents have different boundaries for us that shift as we get older. These boundaries help us understand a lot about the world around us. For example, when my siblings and I were younger, we were taught to spend most of our time at home. Home was where we were safe and could explore our thoughts and ideas without the risk of being in a world where constant changes mean there are no guarantees in life. As we got older and went to school, we experienced new places to develop our ideals and beliefs.

The boundaries our parents set up for us have clues in them that teach us how we can interact with the outside world—as long as we're curious enough to look for these patterns.

Meditation

When you meditate, you're thinking by yourself. This is a time when you work through a process to imagine things that aren't reality *yet*. You can mentally create an alternative existence that is shaped by what you want in life. To me, this was a vital opportunity for reasons you'll see in the next chapter. For now, I want you to know that when you are struggling with present circumstances, meditation allows you to step out of that—even if for just five minutes. It allows you to imagine all that could be. It lets you frame a life that you want, even if you won't be living it until the distant future.

Reflection

Part of my story is that I spent many hours in seclusion due to my accident. This could have been a bad thing, but what it actually helped me to think deeply about the issues that I faced—and that the people I love faced. During this time, my best friends were ants because sometimes they were the only ones around. Looking back now, I realize that the time I was forced to take to reflect on the world around me allowed me to see scarcity as a superpower to activate, not a discouraging force that could stop me from living the life I wanted.

Do you set aside time each day to reflect on your circumstances and opportunities? If not, it's a practice that can change your entire perspective.

When you use both external and internal opportunities to further develop who you are and to better understand your path up to the current point in your life, you will create endless positive possibilities for yourself. The exercise in the next section is just one example of that.

Reset, Restart, Repeat

As you think about where you are right now, I invite you to reset your ideas about the types of internal and external opportunities that exist in your life. That way, you can restart your approaches to them to achieve better results. Follow the instructions below to begin this next part of your development journey.

Opportunity Survey

Create two lists. Make one that names the external opportunities given to you, past and present, and how those opportunities have shaped the way you think about life and yourself. Then, do the same for your internal opportunities.

Now, ask yourself, Are there any opportunities you need to create more time for? For example, do you have the friendships and family relationships you need to feel supported so that you can unlock the benefits from each of the opportunities you have?

If you don't already have a support system made up of people and resources (relationships, education, travel, etc.) that are both internal and external opportunities, what first step can you take to start building that today? Who can you reach out to? If no one comes to mind, think about how you can engage in your community based on external opportunities so that you can build new relationships.

Finally, journal about the answers you discovered as you went through this exercise. Write down a few opportunities you want to add to your life, then choose a few things that are no longer serving you to get rid of.

CHAPTER 2

A Walk Is a Win

I magine that everything you know disappears in an instant. What would you do?

This isn't a question I have to think about in a hypothetical way because this happened to me. Earlier, I shared with you that there is a before and after—the before times and after times surrounding a major accident. This is where you, dear reader, finally see the after times and get a look at how scarcity became a permanent character in my life.

Since I could never completely get rid of scarcity in my life, I needed to learn to leverage it. That is a truth that this moment in my life that I'm about to share forced me to face. There was a miracle at work as scarcity embraced me because instead of meeting an extreme situation with anxiety, my thoughts were shaped by wonder. And that is how scarcity went from being an unwelcome presence to a friend.

The reason I am sharing this fateful event is because I want you to know that whatever happens in your life, you too can face scarcity and create your own tools to leverage it.

Honestly, I don't personally remember a lot of the details of my accident. I was told by my parents and siblings what happened in the event that had the biggest impact on my life. And it went something like this.

My dad was at work, and my mom was at her trade shop in the large, outdoor marketplace. I was left at home with one of the babysitters, but somehow, I managed to sneak out of the house with my brother, the closest to me in age. And since we were both so young, when I decided that I should sneak away from my babysitter to go to school with him that day, he agreed.

I didn't want to sit around and wait for life to happen *to* me. I wanted to make life happen *for* me. Remember, according to my family, that's the kind of person I was in the before times— bundi and ambitious.

Once my brother helped me sneak out of the house, we started walking. His school was on the other side of the big, open market where my mother's shop was, so we started to zigzag through the different booths to make our way across. That's when I saw it.

Coming down the road, there was a white ambulance. Back then, we used wagons—long cars that could hold someone in the back. This one caught my eye because my uncle also had a white station wagon, and I thought the driver was him.

I'm told I broke away from my brother and ran out to greet who I *thought* was my uncle. But it wasn't him, and the driver didn't see me. He was driving at a high speed to pick up someone who needed help. And I must have misjudged how close I was to the car because the wagon hit me—because of the speed, it slammed me good.

I remember just a few things after the impact. I saw people crowding around me. I heard people yelling for my mother, who was on the other side of the market. Eventually, I saw her standing over me. Around me, I kept hearing voices say, "It's your son, it's your son," to my mom and asking, "How did he find himself here?"

I don't know exactly what happened next, but soon, I was inside the same ambulance that had hit me as it drove me toward the hospital. There was a ringing in my ears as we whizzed through the traffic, jolting to the right and left to get around cars. I can't remember who was in the ambulance with me, but the entire ride I thought about my mother's face. The shock I saw in her eyes. The rest is a blur.

When I finally woke up, my family told me that I had been in a coma for weeks. The doctors told my parents that I was going to die. Apparently, my uncle, a man of influence and wealth in our community, made sure that a French doctor came to see about my condition so that this doctor could try to come up with a way to help me.

You see, I had a bad skull fracture and my brain was swollen.

The French doctor told my family that he wanted to perform an experimental procedure on me. I'm still not sure what that experiment was. If I had to guess, I would say that he allowed fluid to leave my brain to reduce the pressure. My parents later told me that up until I had that procedure, I had experienced seizures as a result of the hard blow to my head.

I remember that when I eventually woke up after the procedure, they were draining water from my left ear. Draining, draining, always draining. My eardrum had burst as a result of the accident. But there was more damage in that ear that no one knew about. Something that went unidentified by the doctors. I'll get to that in a bit.

It was bizarre to be awake because I felt like a stranger in my own body. I was weak and disoriented. Every time I tried to sit up or stand up, I felt I would fall down. At first, I didn't recognize my parents or any of my siblings. But I did remember one name: Edith—my sister, closest to me in age—my best friend. I kept asking for her, but not a lot of my family members were allowed into the hospital.

All of my memories had been wiped out due to the trauma. When I looked out the window of my hospital room, it felt like I had become a person who was entering existence for the first time. The vivid thought that kept coming into my head was, "What universe is this, and what world am I on in this universe?"

This was the beginning of my most intense moment of starting over again. Instead of greeting this new world with anxiety, though, my restarted brain looked at what I was going through with a sense of wonder. The new things I was experiencing were exciting to me, so I could unpack and discover each curious item or event without feeling any dread or fear.

Every day, my mother came to reteach me how to walk. I can't remember how many slow steps I took in the hospital hallway with her at my side, coaching me, helping me to stand without falling over. You see, inside the ear, there are extremely small hairs called cilia that help the brain use head movements to determine the direction of gravity. This is a key part of your ability to balance. Now, looking back, I suspect that those hairs, the cilia, were damaged along with my eardrum in the accident.

It was like I was born into the world again as a 4-year-old with a brain that didn't understand anything around me. I didn't know who anyone was. The bird outside my window was a creature I had never seen before. All of the machines around me made noises I didn't recognize. Instead of feeling scared, what I initially felt was a huge sense of curiosity. I didn't know it then, but this was going to be my first personal battle when it came to leveraging scarcity in a world that didn't know what to do with someone like me—someone looking at everything around him like they had literally been born the day before.

From that point on, I was no longer bundi. That ambulance had proven that I was breakable. And I was suddenly thrust into the after times.

Starting Over Again

When I left the hospital, I had a cast on my right hand and strict instructions that my head shouldn't be touched. The top of my head was wrapped tightly because of my skull fracture and the liquid leaking from my ear. I was put inside a taxi, and after that, I remember stepping into our home without any knowledge of this place. That's when I was introduced to everyone in the family for what felt like the first time. My father would say, "This is your brother." And then my mother would tell me, "And this is your sister."

I asked for Edith again, and when I did, my parents pointed at her and said, "She's standing right in front of you." Her face was a stranger's. Even my sister, my best friend, was completely unknown to me.

Instead of feeling discouraged, that sense of wonder for the universe I had felt in the hospital came back to me. This was a chance to rediscover everyone: my father, my mother, my brothers and sisters, our home, and our neighbors. It was a fresh start, and I saw that as a gift.

Scarcity was there, sitting next to me. This time, it was emotional scarcity.

Because of my injuries from the accident, I wasn't allowed to have a normal life. I could no longer run around with other children. I couldn't play sports. And I was asked to stay inside all of the time to keep me safe. Even going for a walk outside was dangerous. Playing with other kids, even my siblings, was out of the question. There was too much at risk: I could stumble and fall and hit my head again—especially with my poor balance. The French doctor had told my parents that if I wasn't careful, I could easily undo the experimental procedure he had done on my skull.

I needed new tools to help navigate this new world. I was fragile, and leaving the house wasn't an option—at least until I started school. And everyone else in my family was busy with things to do: My new inside existence was shaped in a lonely sort of darkness—because we couldn't afford to keep the lights on all day, and there was no one to stay home with me. So I sat by myself in the dim living room.

Slowly, as I began to hear the stories from different family members about where they were when they heard about my accident and how it had impacted them, I realized that I had caused everyone I loved a lot of trouble. That's when I vowed to never cause pain to my family again. That meant it was time to look at what I had and make the best of it.

My desire to keep my family from further difficulties was the motivation that helped me create tools for approaching my situation, where sudden scarcity was thrust upon me because of the accident. A scarcity shaped by the fact that my body didn't work the way it should, and where every single activity posed a danger to my safety.

The first thing I needed to learn to live with was my loneliness—emotional scarcity. But I quickly recognized that I could use my imagination as a tool to create invisible worlds that allowed me to escape the darkness in my lonely house. Even at a young age, I understood how retreating into a world of thoughts and make believe helped me change my situation—even if only for a little while. As an adult, I now realize that what I was doing was reflecting and meditating.

The second opportunity I created for myself happened when I looked around the house to see my one group of constant companions: the ants. They became my new best friends. I had entire conversations with them—often. Because they were the only ones around (my parents and siblings were all at work or school), the ants kept me company and allowed me to feel less alone, even in the midst of the emotional scarcity I experienced.

I was alive, which I was thankful for, but there were still many challenges to face. For example, I couldn't walk straight. Remember the tiny hairs that live in your ear and help your brain figure out gravity? The accident had ruined my balance. I started walking with my head leaning to one side. That was the only way I could take steps forward without falling over.

It was a visual message to the world around me: Max is odd—he's not like the rest of us. That very visible signal was a horrible thing for my parents and siblings to witness. So my parents and siblings were always trying to straighten me out as I walked. I don't think they understood how difficult it was for me to even stand up, and how that strange angle gave me the adjustment I needed not to fall over. And even if they did, I believe they wanted to help me seem less strange—to avoid the judgemental looks and the cultural taboos that surrounded being different.

My father would pray for me every day. My mother too. My siblings also prayed for me constantly. It was really the only thing they could do.

But that walk, as difficult as it was and as strange as it looked, was a huge moment of victory for me. When you can't walk at all and then you can again, a walk is a win.

And my strange walk wasn't even the most difficult part of the after times.

Can't Hear, Can't Touch

Two big things changed about me as a result of the accident: I couldn't hear out of one ear, and I couldn't tell my right from my left.

Not being able to hear out of one ear was something that completely transformed my life. As I got older and started school, the only way I could manage communication was by experimenting. To increase my ability to hear, I would work to hold my head at different angles to see what position best served my situation. I learned to sit at the end of large groups so I could at least pick up some conversation. If I was just with one person, I would make sure to sit on the side where my good ear was, if I could remember which side that was.

But even those efforts weren't enough. Soon, I realized I would need to learn to read lips. I'm sure you can imagine how difficult this was as the language transitioned back and forth from our mother tongue, Baoulé, to French, to a strange mix of the two.

However, I refused to get frustrated and give up because I realized that so much of my life depended on me being able to communicate. Looking back now, I can see that even though I was so young, my accident and the resulting emotional scarcity gave me a superpower that helped me through the aftermath: I had an intense ability to observe others, and that helped me learn how to adjust.

The second problem, that I didn't know my right side from my left, turned out to be what caused constant difficulty. In Côte d'Ivoire, one cannot be left-handed because the cultural taboos around it are extreme. Left-handedness is rare (it affects less than 10% of the entire population), so it is looked at as rude or unwanted, and is associated with bad luck in many African cultures.[1]

---

1   Ayanniyi B. Alhassan, "Left-Handedness and Stigmatization in Africa: Implications for Parents and Teachers," *Global Journal of Archaeology & Anthropology* 7, no. 3, (2018), https://doi.org/10.19080/GJAA.2018.07.555713.

It also wasn't like I could explain what had happened to me. The doctors didn't know why I confused my right from my left other than I had hit my head. My teachers didn't care that the accident had happened. And since I didn't know which side was which, I did things with both hands and often got slapped.

As a result, extreme anxiety followed me everywhere I went. Saying good morning with a handshake was terrifying because I knew I was bound to use the improper hand. And whenever I tried to eat with my left hand, I would get into trouble.

I worried about every conversation, thinking, "What will I do if I can't hear what they are saying?"

Travelwise, the words for right and left meant nothing to me, so getting anywhere by myself was tricky if I hadn't already learned the way to my destination.

When I was 7, thankfully, something amazing happened. I injured my right hand so badly that I was left with a noticeable scar. After that, if I could feel the scar, I knew which side was which. Honestly, sometimes I still can't feel my scar, and I still get confused. Part of me now thinks, in retrospect, that I needed to move to the United States when I was older just so I would be accepted as a left-handed person.

I don't know if I was left-handed before the accident, but in the after times, being left-handed was just the way my brain worked. And I could never really fit in, even at home, with my tendency to use my left hand. In my body, I faced a sort of resource scarcity in that my systems didn't work correctly. And that was about to follow me into a place where not knowing how to do something as simple as writing properly could literally ruin the rest of my life.

Obstacles at School

When I was 5, I started first grade. As soon as I began to attend school—wearing the uniform that had cost important money and urgent, fervent prayers—it became immediately obvious there was something off with my writing. On every assignment I turned in, I would have 40 points marked off for bad penmanship. The truth was, I could write with both hands, and I would get confused about which one to use. And my penmanship was equally bad no matter which hand I wrote with, but at least using my right hand didn't get me slapped.

It didn't matter that I couldn't help how I wrote. It didn't matter that I had experienced a significant brain injury. My teachers didn't want to know anything about me or my accident. They were too busy trying to educate us to actually care about us individually.

This meant that for every paper or test where I got every single answer right, I would still only get 60 out of 100. So I couldn't afford to get any answers to any questions wrong.

At the same time, I could only follow what my teachers were saying for about an hour each day. In that first hour, I expended all of my energy trying to follow along. Remember, I couldn't hear well, and I couldn't write quickly.

Because of the physical and mental toll of my accident, this was a moment in my life when I encountered extreme mindset scarcity. According to my teachers, no matter what I did, it was wrong. That, combined with the regular moments of getting slapped, showed me that unless I figured out how to do things differently, I wouldn't be able to succeed. And to *do* things differently, I first needed to *think* differently.

At the time, I was still learning to read lips, but that was going to take me time—and that meant minutes, hours, and days I didn't have. So, I thought, *Well, if I can teach myself whatever the teacher is talking about, I can still get 60 out of 100 on the papers and tests.* If they weren't willing to care about my situation and teach me in a way that made sense for the way my brain worked, I could still care enough about my situation to keep trying. That's when I first started trying to teach myself.

Back then, I didn't have a word for what I was, but later on, I would learn that I am an autodidact—someone who has the ability to teach themselves without help from a teacher or instructor.

Imagine, dear reader, had I gone through all of school in a normal way and been able to hear my teacher. I would never have learned that I had the ability to teach myself—if scarcity hadn't been my companion. Or had I been able to write with good penmanship, my life would not have turned out the way it has. And you'll see proof of this as we continue with each turn of the page in this book.

It was that character in my life, scarcity, showing up again and teaching me things about myself that I would have never known otherwise. And in ways I would have never expected. Let's look at a few.

The Gifts That Difficult Circumstances Can Bring

One of the biggest obstacles I faced was my difficulty in hearing. Since I couldn't understand what others were saying, I couldn't be active in social groups. As a result, I was known as the weird kid. I didn't fit in with any of my peers. So I spent all of my school hours alone. But there were two huge benefits that happened because I had been socially rejected.

First, because I wasn't invited to join in with the other kids (and I couldn't play anyways because of my head injuries), I spent all of my time observing them. That gave me an opportunity to develop unique perspectives around many ideas that were shaped by the human behavior in front of me.

Second, because I was only really playing by myself, I didn't get into trouble like other kids did. So, over the years, the teachers started to like me. They thought of me as the good kid. And by then, I had learned to pay such close attention to everyone around me that I could read lips and pick up on nonverbal cues. This meant I was able to observe which teacher liked what behaviors—and also understand what each teacher didn't like. It was like I had unlocked a level of understanding that no one else in my school had.

Both of these factors shaped me by helping me become extremely observant about the characters of other people. I could tell when someone was caring and compassionate or when someone was only pretending to be. There were also people who took pride in being mean, and I watched how that shaped their relationships. Because of these observations, I learned how to be empathetic and sympathetic in my communication, and that has continued to serve me throughout my entire life.

All of the difficulties I faced in the after times, what often felt like a hellscape, from first to fifth grade, actually made me into the successful business professional I am today. How? Even in the midst of my loneliness, weirdness, and discouragement, I learned how to use the lack around me, the scarcity, to create tools for myself. And that's what I want for you too.

How to Create Tools From the Scarcity You Face

The first and most important thing to do when you find yourself without something—whether it's a skill or a resource—is to recognize which scarcity your crisis or deficiency is made of. Is it based on emotional scarcity, resource scarcity, or mindset scarcity?

Take a step back and look at the overall situation to gain some perspective. Then you can create a plan to make changes through trial and error, where you attempt different approaches to solving a problem to see which one works best for you and your present situation.

This is the tricky part because in doing so, you are guaranteed to fail. When you are working to respond to scarcity by creating tools, there will be things you try that don't work. But if you keep trying, you will eventually find the tool you need—the thing that provides you with help.

For my hearing, finding a tool meant trying different angles and positions of my head and body that would help me hear better. Or working to learn how to read lips. Or realizing that

I could teach myself, which was important because I couldn't hear the teacher well. Plus, my poor handwriting meant I couldn't take good notes.

But this approach of trying new things to discover a tool that would work isn't limited to me: It will work to help you work through any difficulty you face as well.

And once you find a tool that works, you can use it for your benefit forever. That's why next, we're going to look at the three steps it takes to turn any kind of scarcity into a useful tool.

Step 1: Become Self-Aware

The first step in creating these tools is to *know yourself*.

I understand that this doesn't always feel easy. When you take an honest look at who you are, you might see things you don't like. You will notice areas where you are weak and need to improve. That isn't a fun thing to realize. But, the good news is, you can always adapt by trial and error until you find the tools you need. Tools that can help you overcome whatever weakness you have. And then by using these tools, you can transform yourself.

Self-awareness is important because it is key to acknowledge your personal issues so that you can address them.

Step 2: Identify the Outcome You Want to Reach

Once you've faced the truth about yourself and your situation, you can decide how you want to respond.

If you're struggling with a difficulty like not being able to write well, for example, you can find other ways to communicate.

If you want to become a good student, but you are having a hard time in school, you can develop tools like making time for observing your peers and teachers to help you understand what each one wants, so that you can reach the next level and then the level after that.

What you want to do at this point is choose a goal, but I have a specific meaning in mind when I say that. Let me explain.

The problem we often face when we think about goals is that we try to limit ourselves to the types of goals the world tells us we should have. We look at one big, grand goal, like becoming a CEO, and we don't know how to break it down in smaller steps to get there. If I'm being honest, I know that there are already a million and one books that talk about goals. This isn't one of them (and to be honest, I'm also not the biggest fan of those kinds of books).

Based on my experience, I think the best goal you can set is a small one. Something you can work to do right away. Think about my story. If you're in fifth grade and you want to be a CEO, that's not a goal you can make happen in the present. But learning to read lips to help you communicate better to level up in school, that is something you can work on right away.

Once you know what outcome you want to reach, and you can see how this goal will help you as you work toward your bigger, more long-term goals, it's time for the next step.

Step 3: Try, Fail, & Try Again

This is where trial and error comes in.

Once you have your goal, you need to start experimenting with different ways to make it happen. Like I said earlier in the book, life rarely happens in a straight line. And goals are like that too. The first idea isn't always going to be the best idea. Plus, as you test out different ideas, you're going to have plenty of failures and just a few successes. By failing, what you're really doing is discovering where you need to adjust by seeing what doesn't work, and that gives you valuable information.

However, once you find the tool that works for you, you'll be able to use it to benefit yourself throughout your entire life. That is well worth any starts and stops you have to make along the way. Now, let's take a look at one way we can start to think about the approaches we take to finding tools and adjusting our plans based on scarcity.

Reset, Restart, Repeat

As we move into this section of the chapter, I want to ask you the question we started with:

Imagine that everything you know disappears in an instant. What would you do?

Sometimes, when we think about obstacles that may come into our lives, our brain's first response is anxiety.

Thankfully for me, my default feeling after the accident wasn't anxiety—it was wonder. This allowed me to see the things I could do to change my life, even in the worst circumstances. I could take action to transform my situation, even if those actions started out small.

Who would have ever thought that I would survive being in a dark, lonely house all day by making friends with ants? When I was alone, I could have felt anxious. I could have been afraid. But even in that dark house with the ants, my mind was open and curious about the good things that existed for me in a seemingly discouraging environment, and that is what saved me.

In this exercise, as you think about difficulties you have already faced, I want you to work through the mental process of activating the quality of wonder over anxiety. Because I'm sure you have already overcome some big obstacles to get to where you are now.

This means we need to change the question a little bit.

Imagine back in time to a moment when you faced an obstacle that caused you anxiety. What would have happened if you had embraced wonder rather than anxiety—by looking at the situation differently?

Now, we're going to go through the steps from the previous section of this chapter to take a closer look at how you can create tools from your own scarcity. Grab a notebook or type notes into your computer or phone as we go through this exercise.

What kind of scarcity were you up against? What happened?

Step 1: Become Self-Aware

Were there any deficiencies you had when facing this specific type of scarcity? What was your response emotionally to what happened? Take a look at who you were then: What would you say about yourself as you reflect?

Step 2: Identify the Outcome You Wanted to Reach

As you look back, what would you have wanted to happen as a result of the event that brought that kind of scarcity into your life? What small goal could you have created for yourself in response to that event?

Step 3: Try, Fail, & Try Again

What did you try? What didn't work? What did work? What did you ultimately learn from the adjustments you had to make after you faced that particular difficulty? What tools were you able to develop in response?

And if you weren't able to develop tools at that point, which tools would you want to create now that you have the ability to leverage scarcity by creating tools through this framework?

Amazing job. I am so proud of you for doing this thought exercise. As you'll see in the following chapters, my accident wasn't my only opportunity to develop tools in response to scarcity. I feel like the next part of my story is something that everyone can relate to: the difficulties of middle school.

CHAPTER 3

A Move and a Din

Have you ever felt an overwhelming instinct that something one person thinks is the best for you is actually the worst?

As we move through my middle school career, you are going to see that I experienced that exact feeling. The reason it showed up was because of resource scarcity—and this time the resource I needed more of was time.

As you read on, you'll see me wonder about how I could best leverage time and how I responded when the ability to use time in a way that worked for me was removed. But before I get to time scarcity and how it shaped my life in different ways, I want to share about my unlikely academic success—which I found through the opportunities I recognized along the way.

In life, there are constant internal and external opportunities that present themselves to us. The internal ones come from inside of us and include our mindset. The external ones include things that other people and organizations provide, like education. Both opportunities have value. However, that doesn't mean we will always be excited when they come into our lives. This was the case for me when I moved away from my parents to live with a man I would call my stepfather to go to middle school in the countryside. My mother and father thought that going to this school would present better opportunities for me than the one in our town. In this case, the opportunity came to me in the forms of both resource (time) and mindset scarcity.

Such an abrupt transition was shocking to me, but thankfully, I had already learned a lot from my accident about interpreting the new patterns around me in whatever environment or circumstance I found myself in. The obstacle I faced, though, was whether I could adapt fast enough to make these opportunities work for me instead of against me.

A Move to the Countryside

Leaving my parents was one of the most difficult things I did in my life, and even though I had survived a traumatic accident and the extremely difficult recovery, I was about to be thrust into a different world where I was the littlest fish. When I lived with my parents, I was always a little fish because of my disabilities. But I had a strong support system at home. I had guidance. And I had community in the form of my family.

However, when I started middle school in the countryside, I realized that my differences and disabilities had the potential to make me even more alienated than I had been back home. That was terrifying to me. And as a seventh grader surrounded by both middle school and high school students, I really was the littlest fish. Agewise, sizewise, and otherwise. This is where mindset scarcity came into the picture. I needed to honestly think about *how* I was looking at myself and my situation so that I could make helpful adjustments.

As I walked into my new school for the first time, a big thought followed me around. It was, *All of these kids are older than you. They know more than you do. And they're from a rural background so they won't like how much of a city kid you are. How is this going to go?*

My brother confirmed my greatest fears when, on that first day, he said to me, "Everyone else you see is interested in one thing—they all want to get first place. You have to decide right now who you are going to be here. What is your place among all these people?"

A Din and the Invisible Line

Amazing reader, have you ever heard of the word "din" before? It is a tiny word, only three letters, that represents a vast wall of noise. Because of my hearing difficulties, this wall, this din, threatened to separate me from my purpose in being at the middle school in the countryside. Noise was a constant threat to my understanding, my social standing, and my ability to succeed. And resource scarcity was there behind the scenes, reminding me that I didn't have the same abilities as everyone else.

In order to adapt to my new environment and circumstances, I needed to be willing to walk into that din, the clattering noises of the students around me. And I needed to do my best to blend in. So, I started observing. If I couldn't hear what the students around me were saying because of my limited hearing, I could still watch and mentally document their behavior. Plus, I could read their lips when I was in a smaller group.

The first big thing I noticed was that there seemed to be a separation of people into two groups. An invisible line stood between the city kids and the rural kids. Since we were in the countryside, the students were expected to know how to tend the land, to operate related machinery, and to have an entire dictionary's worth of skills that the city kids just didn't have.

After carefully watching where this invisible line lived, I decided my best bet was to try to cross it. If I was willing to adjust my mindset, I could emulate the way the rural kids talked, acted, and moved. At the same time, I didn't want to lose my city-kid self completely, so I worked to balance who I was—my authentic self—so I could adapt back and forth between city Max and rural Max based on what I thought would give me some belonging in each situation. But at my core, I could still choose to act with integrity and help others.

I didn't want any of the rural kids to see me as a city boy. At the same time, though, I didn't want to be fake because people can tell when you're insincere, and that will cause them to actively work against you. I had seen this happen to other kids, and I didn't want that to be me.

When I thought about the teachers, based on what I had already learned about school, I knew that if I couldn't make the teachers like me and think I was something special, I would never be able to pass all of my classes. So *I* had to believe I was something special. I needed the teachers to look past my bad penmanship and odd ways of sitting and tilting my head so that I could hear them.

The truth is, I knew I couldn't afford to be an outcast again. Everything my parents and siblings had taught me shouted that I wouldn't survive well in the taboos of African culture if I stood out in any big way. In our culture, you have to do your best to fit in because the word "different" is basically another way of saying "wrong."

I also learned something extremely important about myself as I shifted into a new mode in this faraway place: Because of my skills of observation, I could use my personality as a weapon to deflect the fiery arrows of peers who wanted to push me back into that outcast status. I was starting to realize what my tools were and I put them to use right away.

Realizing My Next, Unexpected Goal

Because of everything I had watched and drawn conclusions about in the first few weeks of school, I learned to use my cleverness to sling perfectly-aimed words from within my soul (my personality) to make a difference when someone wanted to defeat me in the schoolyard—socially speaking. I could make my peers laugh at me and forget that I was the target of ridicule. By using empathy, I would notice when other people were in need—and I would use that information to give them a specific type of help. This allowed me to win others to my side. And that approach gave me the ability to learn past what I could observe because it meant others would open up to me. Empathy and a willingness to help were also tools I could use.

I realized that one-to-one interactions with the rural students gave me even more information than what I had gathered when I observed them in groups. By using my personality to endear them to me through kindness and empathy, these individual conversations allowed me to learn the lingo the rural kids used. Plus, they taught me how to clean up a field or hold a certain machine without them even knowing they were acting as my instructors. You could say I learned to use charm to work my way through difficult situations.

Even though I was at a natural disadvantage because of my spatial awareness problems and my hearing issues, I found ways to thrive in this new environment under totally different circumstances by choosing where and when to bring out my true self.

Because of this awareness, I was able to create two different people in myself: the city kid version of Max and the rural kid version. As I lived in both worlds and crossed back and forth over the invisible line, I soon realized I was within reach of getting the thing that every student coveted: the number one academic spot.

That became my new, unexpected goal. And because of the time freedom I had staying with my stepfather (which you'll read more about in a minute), I could create a plan to make this goal a reality.

You see, at one point in sixth grade at this different school in a totally different environment, I took a moment to look at my *new* situation. My stepfather had a cook and cleaners who worked for him regularly, which meant his kids who lived with him didn't have a lot of responsibilities—which meant I could dedicate more time to my studies. My stepfather was a man of power, the kind of man I observed on the bridge that I mentioned in the introduction (a bridge we'll talk more about in this chapter). Because of the life my stepfather had created for himself and those living with him, one of my cousins spent hours each evening studying. In fact, I watched him and realized that he was spending five to six hours each night working on his assignments and learning additional things so that he could get ahead in his studies.

I hadn't initially thought about going to middle school with the idea of becoming excellent in my studies, but I could start to see that it was within my reach. Because of my circumstances and environment, I was set up to succeed, but only because I noticed what was going on around me. I saw how my cousin used all his free time to study and get the top spot in his grade for academic achievement.

To match his accomplishments, the first thing I needed to do was reverse engineer the success my cousin was having: I looked at the results he was getting and looked backward at the path that had taken him there. The thought that lived in my head even in the face of the din at school and kept me motivated was, *I want to go higher*. Soon, I learned that the biggest advantage my cousin had was that he had specific tasks planned out for each hour as he studied. While I watched him and started to create my own list of how to spend each hour after school, I began to see real progress in my own studies. And I also started to realize that no matter where I am or what

I'm doing, I should always have a dream in the back of my mind. I should never be without a dream.

In my first hour, I would review what we did in class. Then, I would do research on a related subject to deepen my knowledge in that area using the books my stepfather had. Next, in my third hour, I would do my homework and try to study ahead based on what I anticipated we would learn in future lessons. Finally, in the fourth hour, I would review the information I went over during the first hour a second time so that I would be better prepared for class the next day.

As I look back, I can see that the structure I added to my homework schedule was a huge help. I had learned how to find information in my earlier years and embraced being an autodidact (self-learner). Even though I tried so hard, I could really only pay enough attention to hear what the teacher was saying for that first hour in class. After that, my brain was too tired to read lips.

While this looked like a disadvantage, I had already learned that if I paid attention to what I was missing—the type of scarcity I was encountering—I could adjust. The same is true for you.

So I looked for the opportunities I had. At school, I encountered resource scarcity in the form of a lack of time. My brain could only focus and help me for so long. However, when it came to my nightly independent study, my hearing difficulties weren't an issue. And because of the focus I found in my hour-by-hour schedule, I was able to make new habits and research every subject we learned to become the best-versed student in each of them—to the point where my teachers couldn't believe my progress.

My stepfather also motivated all of us by saying that he would give us money for each and every A we got in school. He was presenting us with an external opportunity by rewarding us with a financial result that he wanted to see us achieve. One that would address my resource scarcity—as I would be able to buy some of the things I needed. This taught me the seriousness of education. If I worked hard, I could get physical money to buy things I needed. A drive inside of me grew and flourished as I realized I could leverage the resources that my stepfather offered me if I had a strategy in place to get an A in every class.

That time in my life brought one of the most important lessons I've ever learned: Wherever I am, and whatever I'm doing, it is important to always have a dream motivating me in the background, to never leave myself without a dream.

It was through my active imagination and focused work that I was able to learn how to achieve excellence in anything I invested my time in, like school. And from that moment on, dreaming was something that actively transformed my life no matter how many times I needed to start again.

By making sure I was using the resources I had in the environment where I found myself, I was able to move into the number one slot in seventh grade, and I kept that streak running for eighth and ninth grade too. But before I could keep my first-place seat in the upper grade levels, something happened that proved to me that I couldn't leverage scarcity in every environment.

The Rigidity of Boarding School Versus a Broken Brain

Are there ever moments in your life where you look back and think, *Why did someone think that would be a good idea?* That's exactly what happened when my family decided that they were going to enroll me in the boarding school program that was available at the middle school/high school I attended. This meant I would live on campus, where every single second of my time was structured. I didn't have a moment for myself, to build knowledge or to think and wonder about what I had learned. That was when the reality of the lack of time, resource scarcity, started to confront my life in a big way. And while this structure was meant for good and benefited most of the students, it definitely hurt me more than it helped me.

As I entered the eighth grade, I was sent to live in the boarding school complex of my school, which was like a dorm, during the week. There, I was expected to conform to a rigid environment. The idea behind the intense schedule they had for boarding students was based on wanting to maximize the chances for each student's success. They made sure every minute of every day was accounted for with studying, eating, or classes.

Because the school was 45 minutes away from my stepfather's house, my parents, along with my stepfather, decided that the boarding situation would be better for me because they thought it would give me more time to study. Plus, my stepfather wanted to reduce any stress he thought I felt about having to travel back and forth from his house to the school. Because of this lack of independent study time, resource scarcity (since time is an important resource) came for me fast and hard.

Even though I went into the boarding school situation with an open mind, willing to try to make starting over work for me again, this was one of those moments when I faced the reality that I couldn't make *every* situation work with my particular set of limitations.

Every morning, I would wake up in this environment that was like a military camp. At 5:00 a.m., someone was whistling to get you out of bed. That was my first big problem. I couldn't hear the whistle. Or, they were so close with the whistle in my good ear that I became totally overstimulated. It felt like this was a daily nightmare I had entered into against my will.

The next problem was this huge expectation for us to conform, for all of us to do everything the same way in the same amount of time. But I couldn't conform because I was different. My brain was different after the accident. My balance was different from my ear injury. As I already described, my spatial awareness was damaged after I was hit by the ambulance, and that meant when I was marching or doing certain things with the other boarding school students, I got confused and would make mistakes.

In the midst of all of this, I had to completely give up my study schedule. It felt almost impossible to succeed. Suddenly, I was expected to learn the content in class, and I didn't have time to teach myself to make up for what I couldn't hear. And because I lost some of what had made me special in the eyes of my teachers—my grades went down and my class interactions weren't adding new information to our discussions—I had a more difficult time winning the teachers over. I could no longer depend on my personality to get them to look past my poor penmanship because they no longer saw me as exceptional in their subject. Because I didn't have time to learn anything extra, I had nothing new to add to our class discussions.

Something else also happened as a result of this environment: I didn't have time or a place to dream. I couldn't spend time imagining my future and what it could be because I didn't ever have a spare minute to myself.

There are people who totally thrive in the structured environment of a boarding school, but I couldn't. I ended up having to do everything twice or three times. Every assignment, every task. Even something as simple as shaking hands to say good morning made me look like I couldn't complete basic things because often I couldn't remember which hand was right and which was left.

All the accomplishments I had worked hard to earn through my grades and reputation—by overcompensating for my disabilities—were threatened. I felt like all my goals and dreams were about to completely disappear because unlike the other students, I could not attain the conformity the school wanted me to have because of my disabilities.

Sometimes, the best way to leverage scarcity is to realize that a specific brand of scarcity—in this case for me it was the resource scarcity of time—cannot be leveraged. This experience taught me that I needed to be more than just a fast action taker; I needed to be a fast quitter in the face of unhelpful scarcity as well. I had to be willing to pivot.

It was time to tell my family that the schedule of the boarding school wasn't helping me—it was hurting me. As hard as I worked to make what could have turned into an opportunity into a benefit for myself, I couldn't. I needed my own schedule and my own time every day to help my brain learn what it needed to understand. Living at school was not allowing me to do that.

Thankfully, my parents listened when I told them the boarding program wasn't working out after just a year. They saw how I had tried to honor their wishes and leverage the situation they thought would help me—even though it hadn't worked out as they had hoped. As a result of our talk about what was happening to me as I lived on campus, they decided to send me back to my stepfather's home.

Staring Across the Bridge and Dreaming Again

I will tell you, dear reader, that boarding school almost killed the spark to strive for excellence that I had worked to grow inside of myself.

But there were moments when I stopped on the bridge between my stepfather's house and the school I went to where I felt like my soul was able to grow. And then, when I went home to be with my parents, being back with the people I loved in an environment that felt safe and supportive gave me the room to dream again. And not just normal dreams. Big, inflated ones that allowed me to picture myself becoming anything I wanted to be.

During that year, I stepped into a special season of dreaming in my life. A season of dreaming that I mentioned in the introduction of this book—which had started when I would stand on the bridge to look at the CEOs and politicians being driven around the city in their fancy cars.

This wonderful bridge, the place where I could imagine a different life for myself, was about an hour and a half walk both ways from my stepfather's home. But I was willing to make that journey countless times if it meant I could have my dreams back—the ones that had almost disappeared because of boarding school.

The bridge overlooked the river, and while cars drove along the middle of the bridge, there was also a pedestrian side. This bridge held the main road that people would need to travel on to enter or leave town. And it was really the only way to get to the airport.

My friend and I would meet there and talk about the fancy cars with chauffeurs that would drive by. We would promise each other that someday we would dress in fancy clothes like these men. That we would be able to wear suits and ties and look high status whenever we needed to go someplace important in the world.

From our place on the side of the bridge, we also saw the United Nations convoys in fancy vehicles. We also saw the man who was like our governor at the time. We even saw Charles Taylor, the former president of Liberia, who later ended up in jail after being sentenced by the Special Court for Sierra Leone to serve 50 years for committing war crimes.

Walking an hour and a half in the heat to go to this special place might seem like a lot, and it felt that way on some days. But every bead of sweat and every sigh of effort I spent getting there was worth it—to visit the special place where my dreams could soar and fly high.

As you've seen in this chapter, the key to getting through the difficult times I faced in middle school was being aware of my environment and observing what I could do to leverage scarcity in my new circumstances. And to understand when a specific brand of scarcity wasn't going to help me, which is what happened with the resource scarcity of time in the boarding school.

If you understand your limitations and find a tool that helps you to move past them, that's when you can really succeed. Boarding school couldn't do that for me. This is a lesson I have taken with me to countless places, and now, I want you to take it along with you so that you can face whatever you do, wherever you go. Because you also deserve for *your* dreams to soar and fly high. And even when you find yourself in difficult situations or new environments, you can still find a way forward.

Start Over Again to Win—Observe Your Surroundings

I thought about the different kinds of scarcity I could leverage when I started middle school. That's when I realized that while I was there, I had resource scarcity in the form of time. Aside from that, I had plenty of resources, really for the first time in my life. So, by combining what I could leverage from the scarcity I experienced with the resources I had, I was able to create a plan. I was able to set goals. And those goals helped me leverage the mindset scarcity I faced.

When I talk with young people these days, one thing that I notice is that they often neglect to set specific goals. They might say, "I want to go to college," but they don't know what they will do with the degree they earn. Or they might say, "I'm working at this shop temporarily, and eventually I'll do something else with my life," but they aren't actively working toward a specific dream.

And I understand why. Allowing yourself to dream and to set goals that you might not be able to reach is scary. However, at the same time, if you don't dream and if you don't set specific goals, you won't be able to work toward something that gives your life meaning and purpose, and that would be a real shame.

You are full of potential! And as you work your way through this book, you are learning to look scarcity in the face—to acknowledge it and use it. And that's not a skill most people are willing to develop.

Because of how amazing and capable you are (and are continuing to learn to become), I want to give you a formula that will help you realize and prioritize your own goals and dreams. Are you ready?

Dream the Dream, Set the Goal

Follow these simple directions to start allowing your mind to go to an imaginary place in the future. In this case, you are going to learn how to leverage mindset scarcity by being honest about what you really want.

Step 1: Build the Dream

Close your eyes, take a deep breath, and name four things that you want in this lifetime.

For example, I knew that I wanted to be able to provide resources for my future family and that gave me the idea of making it a goal to move to the United States where I would have many more external opportunities than I would in my own country.

Step 2: Observe Your Present Reality

Now that you have a list of some of the things you most intensely desire, compare those dreams to your current life. Are there differences between what you dream of and what your current situation is? Take time to identify those differences.

When thinking about my goal of moving to the United States, I knew that my best bet was to get a student visa, so making sure I got top academic marks became one of my smaller long-term goals. All so that my application looked good when I tried to get that type of visa.

Step 3: From Dream to Goal

Think about your reality and the dreams you've just identified. Even though you might not have been consciously working toward a specific dream, you have probably already set some things in motion around that dream. Identify which one of your dreams is the closest to your reality right now. That is going to be your first goal. Write that one down. That is the goal we're going to focus on for the rest of this section.

In order for you to start over again to win—to turn your first goal into reality—one of the biggest things you need to do is to observe your surroundings. This is how you can leverage all three types of scarcity: emotional scarcity, mindset scarcity, and resource scarcity. Because when you examine what is around you and what is missing, you will see which changes need to happen so that you are able to build a path that allows you to realize your goal.

You can use the following questions to help you evaluate your environment to see what is available to you and what is not— which will show you what you need to find. Think through each question and how your answer relates to your new goal. Write down everything you discover as you work through this process.

- If my environment is one I'm used to, what new things can I observe as I look through the new lens of my specific goals? If I am in a new environment, what do I notice that can help me?
- What am I not used to as I look around me, and how can I make up for those things in relation to the new goals I have?
- How can my current surroundings support me as I go after my goal?
- What resources do I have to achieve that goal?
- Which people, who present me with external opportunities, can help me accomplish my goal?

- Do I have the mindset that will help me in this environment, or do I need to adjust my mindset?
- What emotional support do I have as I work toward my goals under my specific set of circumstances?
- Do I need to build additional emotional support for myself? If yes, how will I go about doing that?

Now that you have your answers, I want you to make two lists. Write down all of your internal opportunities (that come from your own knowledge, mindset, imagination, and family) and your external ones (that come from what is outside of you like education, government programs, and community-shared knowledge and resources). Then, make a list of the opportunities you need to complete your goal but don't currently have.

For example, when I was striving for excellence in middle school, I had the resource of my cousin's homework schedule that I used to help me achieve the goal of getting the highest grades in my class.

Take the Leap

When I was studying at the middle school, another resource I had was my ability to observe the invisible line that existed between the city kids and the rural kids. From watching the way people behaved and learning what *I* needed to succeed in that particular environment, I recognized that I would need to travel back and forth over that invisible line if I really wanted to become first in my class, pursuing my goal of wanting to go higher.

But solely observing what was going on around me wasn't enough to actually change my life. I had to figure out how to put what I had learned about my environment and the people around me into action. That required me to take a leap of faith because I wasn't sure that what I wanted to accomplish was going to work out. But when I took that leap, that's when I started to see real results.

Dreaming isn't enough to change your reality. You also have to take action.

The next section is to help you understand what it means for *you* to take the leap. To take action. And then, in the next chapter, we're going to look at how the people around you can create external opportunities that will help you leverage the scarcity in your life.

Reset, Restart, Repeat

In this next exercise, I want you to treat your current circumstances as if you are just encountering them for the first time. This mindset reset will help you see both the opportunities and types of scarcity those circumstances offer you with fresh eyes to give you a different perspective on what your response could be.

My Mindset Reset

Step 1: Observe your new environment. What natural advantages do you have? What disadvantages can you spot?

Step 2: Identify one to three specific goals you have as you engage with the circumstances you currently face.

Now, in the next two steps, you're going to create a response plan that will help you understand which actions will bring you closer to your goals.

My Response Plan

Step 3: Create the first part of your response plan based on the advantages offered and your strengths. What do you need to do, using the skills you currently have, to work toward the goals you created in the previous step?

Step 4: Work on the second part of your response plan based on the scarcity you face and your natural disadvantages. What skills or resources do you need to build in order to reach the goals you wrote down in step 2?

Step 5: As the last piece of your response plan, write down the internal and external opportunities you have as you work to accomplish your goal. This includes making a list of all the people you need to work with or perhaps gain access to in order to make your goals into reality.

For example, to achieve my goal of excellence in school, I needed to find a way to connect with the rural kids so that I could learn what they knew to do well in school. Without the opportunities they gave me, I never would have been able to secure that first spot in my grade.

Once you have your response plan, put it somewhere that you can see it and choose one action to work on at a time until you accomplish everything on the plan.

CHAPTER 4
Stepping Together With Them

As we start this chapter together, I want to share with you one of the most important concepts I've learned in life: When you are alone—or even in a group but you choose to stay silent—it is impossible to leverage scarcity. But when you are active in a community and use your voice to stand up for others and use your actions to cultivate an attitude of giving back, that is extremely *contagious* to those around you. And this is one of the best ways to leverage resource and emotional scarcity by using external opportunities.

It was through this lesson that I realized how important it is for each one of us to be part of a community.

In my life, scarcity was my constant companion. At the same time, leadership also became a fast friend. In the previous chapter, you found me in middle school. Well, in my final year, both scarcity and leadership teamed up to give me an opportunity to learn exactly what I was made of. In this chapter, you will learn how through my desire to impact the community of students around me, I found my authentic voice. In this case, I used my voice to say, "No," so that I could leverage resource scarcity for the students around me. Let's take a look at what happened.

The Carnival of Character

During my last two years of middle school (eighth grade in the boarding program and ninth back at my stepfather's house), a unique opportunity presented itself. People told me that I had enough influence to run for student council. So I first became the president of my class. That was an enjoyable experience, and as I started to learn skills that allowed me to be an effective leader for others, I realized I wanted to do more. I wanted to go higher, again. And I began to recognize that one of the best ways to do that was to go together with others so that we could all contribute our individual skills and gifts to whatever we were working on.

As the African proverb goes, if you want to go fast, go alone; if you want to go far, go together.

That's why in ninth grade I decided to run for treasurer of the entire school. And I won! After all of those moments I had spent feeling like an outcast among my teachers and fellow students, this felt like a huge victory. And it was because of this experience that I realized what kind of person I would choose to be. Let me explain.

Every year, the school held a carnival to make money to cover the in-school expenses of the student body. I worked hard to set up the different systems we needed to collect ticket money and reconcile all of the funds gained as a result of the ticket sales. But then, on the day of the carnival, the student body president came up to me with a serious look on his face.

"Hey," he said, "the way this works is that now that all of the proceeds of the carnival have been added up, we take half of it and split it among ourselves. Since we are the only ones who report how many tickets we sold, we can just say that we sold half of what people really purchased and give that half to the school—while we keep the other half of the money. We've done it before and so far no one has found out."

"What?" I said. "That's not right. I won't do that."

"This is the way it always works, and whether or not you want your cut, I'm still taking half of the money," he said, trying to sway me.

"Over my dead body!" I said, "The students need this money, and it is rightfully theirs."

The president could see how serious I was, and even though he was clearly annoyed with me, he backed down. As a result, I succeeded in making sure that all of the money made it into the student fund.

That was a moment in my life when I could have chosen to better my own situation by embezzling from others. In a split second, I responded without even having to think about it. In that moment I remember having the realization, *Well, I guess this is who I am. This is the kind of person I'm going to be: A man with integrity.* By watching my own actions, I was communicating to myself that my strong integrity is part of my character. That was a pivotal point in my development.

Have you ever experienced a defining moment like that?

When we observe our environments, like we talked about in the last chapter, we have opportunities to decide which actions we will take. And those decisions shape who we will become long term. With the carnival, I was willing to say no to the dishonest intentions of the president and allow him and the other student council members to perceive me as weird. If I had taken part in his scheme, no one outside of the student body leadership would have known, but I would have had to live with that.

The truth is, because of that ever-present character in my life, scarcity, a different choice might have been tempting, as I was in a situation where I had several disadvantages. That money would have really helped me out. But I was able to create a path forward for myself without stealing. And you can too, no matter what circumstances you were born into. You don't have to be a part of taking from those around you: You can choose to have integrity. You have the choice to improve the world around you. That's the gift of leveraging scarcity. Especially resource scarcity.

Because when you say no to resources that weren't found or created in an honorable way, you are able to leverage mindset scarcity (which means that you are proving to yourself who you are and improving your mindset by taking integrity-based actions). When you do dishonest things, you are proving to yourself that who you really are is someone that lacks integrity. This only makes mindset scarcity worse.

As you'll see in the next section, this was just the beginning of my friendship with the presence of leadership, and like the presence of scarcity, leadership helped me realize that I could make the world a better place by showing up and teaching others how to leverage mindset scarcity to improve their integrity. And what a valuable relationship leadership and I still have today!

Learning to Leverage Resource Scarcity by Engaging the Community in a Positive Way

After I finished tenth grade, my family brought me home to live with them in Abidjan, away from my stepfather, my cousins, and the reputation I had built at the school there. All so I could go to high school near them. As it turned out, the hard work I did in middle school paid off because when I was tested, I was offered a scholarship to go to a fancy school near where my parents lived (which I'll share more about in a bit). But there were all kinds of problems for me when it came to actually getting to school, having what I needed, and being able to thrive.

First, there was the problem of actually getting from my house to the school itself. This required taking the public bus system. And that meant I needed bus money for each and every school day, both going and coming.

Next, I needed school supplies like books, notebooks, pens, and pencils. I couldn't manage my classes without them, and my family just didn't have the resources to provide them for me. I was on my own.

Then, there was the basic need for food. The truth is, I spent most days at school starving, with no lunch prepared for me due to the lack of food at home. And it really affected my ability to think. If I wanted to thrive in class, that was a need I absolutely had to address.

The final problem I had came at the end of each school year: I had to face summer. For me, it wasn't fun to take time off school. And I was nervous for me and my friends, especially when I thought about how we would use the down time when we weren't busy with classes. From experience, I knew that bored teenagers often meant trouble. But before I could address the summer problem, I needed to figure out how to survive the challenges of the school year.

Scarcity, that ever-existing presence in my life, was showing up in a big way when it came to the resources I needed, and the gap between those needs and what I actually had was big.

This was a season in my life when I really needed help, and part of that help came in the form of reading my Bible each and every day. It was during this practice that I got to know God more and more, and I would pray and cry out to him about the different problems I was facing. And as I prayed, I also knew that I needed to prepare myself for what I was facing in light of the educational opportunity God had clearly given me.

Here is how everything happened.

Problem 1: No Money for the Bus

When I first came back home, I felt like a complete stranger to the community around me. Sure, I had been home for the summer months each year, but I hadn't worked to maintain any of the relationships I had before I left. Plus, when I moved to my stepfather's, I had been so young that I hadn't had the maturity to build relationships with the adults in the community where I had originally grown up. But I needed to develop those relationships that would become pivotal for me (as you're going to see later).

As I evaluated my situation, I realized that I needed to build a new life in this community. First, I knew it would help me to know the adults who lived nearby—I had seen relationships shape my ability to succeed through getting my teachers to like me in middle school. Plus, I looked at the other kids around me who I knew I wanted to lead and help (based on what I had been able to do through the student council at the middle school). To do that, I needed to work with the adults who were key players around me.

You see, when I had helped the students back in middle school by making sure they got *all* of the money from the carnival instead of half, I learned just how important helping others was to me. This was a new mission in my life.

As I worked to start building those relationships, I was given an amazing opportunity. There was an area in the city somewhat near me that made me think of Beverly Hills in California because this city also had a private school for gifted people with intellectual abilities. After I passed the middle school exam with super high marks, this bougie school invited *me* to go there on a scholarship.

Like I said earlier, all of those hours I spent studying in middle school had seemed to pay off. However, there was one big catch. While the school had given me a scholarship, meaning I wouldn't have to pay for tuition, I still had to find my own way there every day. But since it was physically further from me than my local school, the only reasonable way to get there was by using public transportation. That meant bus fare was needed twice a day—yet again.

I agreed to attend the not-so-close school, certain that I could find a way to get the money I needed each day to make it to school and back. When I thought about the big picture of my life, I knew that going to such a prestigious school would help me in the future. This scholarship was a huge external opportunity that I knew I couldn't pass up.

So there I was, going to this bougie high school and not really being able to afford the related costs—even with the scholarship that paid my tuition. My first thought was that I could go to my brothers and sisters for help, observing the resources I might have in my family to help me solve my problem. I figured that even if only a few of them gave me enough money for one trip of bus fare, that would be a big help.

Next, I went to the "uncles" and "aunties" in my community. People in my neighborhood. If they knew my brothers or sisters, there was a higher chance they would be interested in helping me with my education. I didn't realize it at the time, but I was leveraging resource scarcity by using the relationships and connections my family members had made while I was away at school. All I had to do was talk to my siblings about who they knew and go from there.

Plus, because I was interested in helping my community, I took every chance possible to do good for these "uncles" or "aunties," whether that was the gift of a positive conversation and spending time with them or asking them if they needed help and responding accordingly.

And the thing is, my investments didn't cost me anything but time and effort and would prove to go a long way in helping me complete my education. How? As I showed friendship to those around me, they returned it by becoming invested in my future (many times by giving me bus fare). They also learned that I wouldn't use what they gave me to buy cigarettes or alcohol—because I was super focused on using whatever resources I had toward furthering my education.

I also asked my parents to help me find available support through the government. As far as I was concerned, I was going to leave no resource untouched. This brings me to my next problem.

Problem 2: No Money for School Supplies

Even though there were days I went to school not knowing how I would find the money for bus fare home and I was okay with that, not having any school supplies was a different story. I needed pencils, paper, and notebooks—just the basic things. But those costs added up fast, so I needed to plan ahead for that money as much as I could.

My sisters worked the hardest to make sure I had what I needed, but what they couldn't provide would often be given to me by some of the wealthy kids at my school.

Once I started classes, I noticed quickly that some of the other kids were in the same situation as me—they were lacking resources. But the other kids lived in the bougie neighborhood around the school, meaning they were rich and had more than enough resources. So it didn't really cost them much to share their supplies with me. The only thing they required in return was a friend who actually cared about them, and I was thankful to have the opportunity to be just that for those people. I would have done that for them even if they hadn't shared pencils and pens with me.

For the most part, I didn't really need to ask them for help. If they saw I needed something, they would usually offer it to me. That was a huge blessing and helped me keep my dignity in a difficult situation.

However, there was one need that most people couldn't see.

Problem 3: A Grumbling Stomach

Physical hunger is one of the most difficult things that any person can deal with. It creates feelings that all three types of scarcity bring up. There is the emotional scarcity related to the fact that someone has neglected to care for you by providing you with food—whether that was intentional or was a direct result of the circumstances of the family. In my case, of course my parents wanted to provide food for us, but the budget just wasn't there. Then, there is resource scarcity of food, one of the most basic resources that any human needs. When you don't have it, multiple levels of suffering happen. And that leads to mindset scarcity. Let me ask you, dear reader: Have you ever tried to focus on learning something when your stomach was audibly growling? When you felt pangs of pain from your body desperately shouting to you that it needs food?

If yes, then you know how intensely your mindset can suffer when you don't have the nourishment you need.

Scarcity taught me how to use hunger as a motivation to build better relationships. At school, there were kids who knew my situation and shared their food. But there were also days when not one person would offer me a morsel of anything. I had to sit and pretend that I was fine—that I wasn't hungry. And that was so difficult. I felt the pressure to act like the kids who lived in that area without any need, whose parents were wealthy professors or doctors.

At some point, I realized that I could reach out to people in the community around the school. During my lunch break, I would go and offer to sweep out different shops. Or sometimes, I would just show up and listen to the stories of the shop owners or "uncles" that worked in the neighborhood around the school. Since it was lunch time, they would regularly offer to get me something to eat or take me out to lunch.

On those days—days when I had food in my belly—I could better focus in class. And all because of the generous hearts of the people around me. I never felt like they owed me anything, even if I did small jobs or chores from them. But I was thankful whenever they shared something with me.

And while I took on each of these three problems as best as I could—while leveraging my scarcity by serving others and building better relationships with those around me—the problems I was solving at school were different than the ones I wanted to fix at home. Especially when it came to helping my local friends who were around my age.

Problem 4: Boredom Getting My Friends Into Trouble

As summer came again and the risk of boredom became real, when I looked at the resources available to the kids with wealthy parents—both in my middle school where my stepfather lived and in the neighborhood where I had earned a scholarship to the bougie school—I noticed a huge difference between what those kids had and what my friends at home had. That caused a lot of emotional distress for me.

I knew that if we had activities for the local kids to participate in during summer, they would be less likely to let boredom sway them into activities, like partying and damaging property, that would get them into trouble.

So, I created a community club, inspired by the Rotary Club and the Lions Club. We would gather each day to make plans for community events, do clean ups in the neighborhood, and help out local business owners whenever we could. I was also inspired by the fact that there were other people in different cities doing something similar for the local youth.

Once I got everyone together, we would brainstorm about what kinds of events we could host. We would start preparing in June so that we could be ready to host the first community-inspired event in July and then another in August. Let me tell you what those events looked like.

First, we created a community beautification committee and enlisted the help of local business owners and community leaders who would either donate cleaning supplies or their time to help. The goal was to make our neighborhood look and feel better. Next, we held a beauty pageant to help the young women in our community build their confidence. And local businesses offered support by donating items we needed for prizes.

Looking back now, I see that through those experiences, I learned how to ask others for help. And I taught the other young people in our group to do so as well. We needed money and materials to host the different events in our community, and that meant we needed to go door to door to make those things happen. I didn't know exactly what I was doing, but talking to adults and encouraging them to partner with us taught me that asking was important. I thought, *What is the worst thing that can happen? They say no. I can always still ask someone else for help if the first answer is no.*

By pushing myself and encouraging others to leverage the scarcity we faced as a community, using the relationships we had to make our neighborhood better, I realized that we could fake it until we made it. This meant that if we didn't have the skills we needed, we could always try. If we failed, then we could observe the missing pieces that we needed so we could learn how to fill those in. And at the same time, I was building leadership skills and confidence that I still use to this day.

Plus, my original motivation of creating exciting community-based opportunities for my friends worked. During that summer, no one was bored, and so no one got into trouble trying to solve that boredom. Then, it was time to go back to school.

Stretching My Leadership Wings

During the next academic year, I worked as a spokesperson for the 50th anniversary of our establishment. The principal would drive me around to radio shows and TV stations where I would share about the celebration weeks and how much the school appreciated the community's support.

As I continued to stretch my leadership wings, I began to learn how far they could take me. That was a lesson I would desperately need in the coming years. One of the most important ways I learned to lead was by looking at those around me to find out who would be vital in helping me and the people I was close to. It was through leveraging these valuable relationships that I made it through high school, which you can see, was where I was accompanied by my ever-present companion, scarcity. It has consistently been the character of scarcity in my life that helped me learn how beneficial it is to ask for help. And scarcity taught me to ask curiosity-based questions so that I could find more context in any situation. Plus, scarcity taught me that one of the most important things I could do was ask for help.

Through asking, I learned just how valuable the community around me could be and how we could make the lives of each other better. Firsthand, I saw that the African proverb is true: I went further together with the people who said yes to helping than I could have ever gone alone.

But it's not easy to ask for help, is it? In the next section, we're going to talk about why that's true, and then I'm going to share my ASK framework. Because even if it feels scary at first, your brain can be convinced that asking others to assist you is a really important thing to do.

Convincing Your Brain It Is Okay to ASK for Help

Over the years, I've noticed that one of the most difficult types of scarcity is related to our mindset. Even when we know that we need help, we often refuse to ask for it because our mind says, *What if our asking makes the other person feel awkward? Or, Unless I do everything myself, I'm a failure.*

The reason our minds do this is to protect us from what our brains analyze as unnecessary risk. Our brain can actually mark these kinds of interactions as a physical threat, which is why it is so difficult to leverage mindset scarcity. Our minds analyze situations that aren't life-threatening but can easily identify these same circumstances as creating risks our brains don't think we should be taking.[2]

In order to leverage mindset scarcity, you have to understand that it requires a mental battle to overcome anything your brain sees as a risk. And in this specific case, you need to learn how to ASK others for help, even when your mind doesn't want you to.

---

2 "What Is the Fight, Flight, Freeze or Fawn Response?," Cleveland Clinic, July 22, 2024, https://health.clevelandclinic.org/what-happens-to-your-body-during-the-fight-or-flight-response.

This is why I have created the ASK framework: to help you combat your brain to leverage the three different types of scarcity you face, emotional, resource, and mindset—but especially mindset scarcity.

The ASK Framework

There are three key things to do when you're trying to convince your brain to ASK for help:

1. Act with authenticity.
2. Step through your fear.
3. Keep your vision at the center.

Now, let's take a look at each step of the ASK framework.

Act With Authenticity

If you are acting solely out of self-interest, the people you approach to ask for help will know. This will create a strong mental block for them because most of us don't want to help someone who seems selfish since asking for help with only yourself in mind can look manipulative.

So, before you make your ASK, think about the following questions:

- Am I coming from a place of service as I approach this person? Or is my motivation selfish?
- Do I genuinely care about this person, our connection, and making their life better through the way I interact with them—beyond just getting help for my specific needs?

When you focus on authenticity in your motives and work to show the person you're asking for help respect, your brain won't see asking as a manipulative act. And neither will their brain. This is how you leverage resource scarcity and emotional scarcity: View those around you as people you want to help and remind yourself that if they say no, it's just part of the process. That doesn't mean that relationships are damaged. The effort you put forward will actually help you build meaningful relationships. The truth is, real help comes when you both care about each other.

You can always build deeper relationships—but your intention has to be pure, and your interest in the other person has to be real. This is the foundational step in the ASK framework, but there are two more to walk through.

Step Through Your Fear

Fear will tell you, "Don't ask because they might say no."

But courage says, "What good will come by asking if they say yes?"

While many people (and minds that are motivated by scarcity) will say that if you ask for help, you're being entitled, I don't think that's true. When you ask for help, knowing that you also plan to help the other person in whatever way you can, that is not being entitled. In this case, I would say that asking is an act of bravery. When you choose to be brave, you are leveraging mindset scarcity by telling your brain, *Yes, I understand this is a little scary, but I can do this, and it will benefit both me and others.*

Here are three reasons why it makes sense for you to step through your fear to ASK for help:

1. You are showing how strong you are when you step forward boldly to get help—making an ASK is *not* weak.

2. In the worst-case scenario, you get a no. But in the best-case scenario, you get a yes, and that can be life-changing.

3. Nothing is going to change for you or the people you want to help unless you take action.

One of my older brothers has always been a particularly intelligent man and hard worker, but he was intimidating to all of us younger siblings. However, one of my sisters and I knew that as students in certain situations, he could help us. So we would ask him for help—even though it felt scary. We even had a song about it. We would sing, *Il faut tenter ta chance, faut laisser avoir peur*, to pump ourselves up before asking him for something. Loosely translated, this means, "You have to try your luck, and don't let fear take over."

Our dreams of being successful students were more important than our fear of asking him for help. And often, when we were brave and asked him for school supplies or bus money, he would say yes. Finally, let's look at the third step in the ASK framework, when we remember our motivations.

Keep Your Vision at the Center

When you are working to convince your mind that the risk of asking is one worth taking, it helps to remind your brain of what you are working to achieve. If you get help, you can leverage resource scarcity to get the objects you really need. There are two compelling reasons to make an ASK:

1. To pursue your dream.
2. To live out your individual purpose.

These two motivators are powerful because they help you focus on what you're working toward. This step reminds you of *why* you're asking—instead of you thinking solely about *what* you're asking for.

Your dream and your purpose will fuel your courage. When I was asking for $20 for bus fare, I wasn't just asking for bus fare. I was asking for help taking another step toward my dream by working to further my educational opportunities. That was extremely motivating for me.

If as you work through the ASK framework, you still find it difficult to find the courage to ASK, I want you to visualize the joy, the growth, and the wow that will happen when your dream becomes real.

When you ASK in connection to your purpose, your brain will stop identifying asking questions as a threat or risk because the results will allow your mind to see that you're working to create something that's bigger than just yourself.

Now, let's put this framework into practice as you work to leverage scarcity in your own life.

Reset, Restart, Repeat

Create a journal entry where you explore the answers to both of these questions:

1. When was the last time I *wanted* to ask someone I trust for help but felt too scared to follow through?

2. How can I use the ASK framework to convince my brain that asking isn't actually risking my life? How can this framework help me take courageous action to get the help I need in the future?

Now, create an ASK goal based on your dreams or purpose and answer the following questions.

1. What do you need help with?

2. How can you use the ASK framework to get that help from someone you authentically care about building a stronger relationship with?

The next time you need help, you can use this framework to determine who you are going to ask for help from. And if they say no, then you can just repeat the process again with someone else until you find someone who says yes.

CHAPTER 5

Not With You Then

Dear reader, as we've traveled through this book together, I've told you about how after the accident with the ambulance, the concept of wonder was my default. That's what changed the way I looked at the character of scarcity in my story. But in this chapter, wonder was *not* my default. Shock followed by numbness became my reality—after I suffered what I still consider to be the greatest loss in my life. And no, I'm not talking about my accident.

Why was wonder not my default? And how did numbness become my reality? Those are questions I'm going to answer soon, but as we begin on a new path of our journey together, I want to start by saying that sometimes, there is no choice but to stop going after your vision. And that's okay. Let me explain.

There is a specific kind of scarcity that is ruthless. That kind of scarcity, the one I want to talk about in this chapter, is grief. It combines different elements of what we've learned so far in that it causes intense scarcity on all three levels. It depletes your emotional resources by plunging you into a deep sorrow.

It removes resources in that all of the information you had stored in an important loved one is gone—everything they knew about life and about you, your story, and your strengths.

Grief also plays havoc with your mindset because you've lost one of your most important cheerleaders. You can no longer hear their belief for you in the present—because that beloved, encouraging voice will never speak words on this side of heaven again.

Grief is the ultimate form of scarcity, creating deficits in every area of life.

And as much as I want to tell you that yes, even the scarcity of grief can be leveraged—if I say that without acknowledging what kind of vicious beast this kind of scarcity can become, then I'm not helping you. I'm hurting you.

This part of the story finds me, young Max, recently having graduated from high school. All of the skills I had been able to leverage and create ended up with me testing well in my exit exams and being sent off to law school. To a city where I didn't have any relationships or resources. I was starting over, yet again.

Observing My New Situation

I had never really thought about becoming a lawyer, except when I was on that bridge above the river as dignitaries and businessmen passed by on the middle road while I dreamed about my future. But when it came time to see what was possible based on my test results, learning about the law felt like a way to get into one of those cars driven around by a chauffeur. Or so I thought.

However, at the first university I went to, I didn't really have any resources. There wasn't anyone I knew who could help. And, to add to the stress, because of political issues, the campus had remained closed as a response to student protests which prevented me from going to class. If I continued to study there, it was going to take me two to three times as long just to finish what I had started—and without the support I really needed. I definitely could not afford to pay for any extra years of tuition.

That's why, for my second year of study, I transferred to a law school in Bouaké, where one of my sisters lived. Her husband *was* one of the people being driven around by a chauffeur. And staying with her meant not only that I would have help with basic needs like food but that I would have someone to cheer me on with my courses. At the same time, it gave me the chance to encourage my sister during my weekend breaks when she graciously opened her home to me. This also meant I could avoid the political issues that kept my previous campus closed.

It felt like a win, win, win.

What I didn't know at the time was that I needed to be in that exact geographic location to confront scarcity coming for me, yet again—this time as the most intense form of scarcity, grief.

During my second year of university, my mother came from Abidjan to Bouaké (the same city my sister lived in where I was attending university) to visit because her aunt had died. My mother had grown up in Bouaké and many members of her family still lived there, including my maternal grandmother.

Even though my mother was geographically close, I didn't expect to see her because she was in her home village and planned only to be there for a short trip to attend the funeral. Little did I know what was coming next.

Come Quick, Something Is Wrong

After the funeral, my sister got a call from my mom's family. Then, my sister called me to say that our mother had passed out, and the family wanted us to come quickly since we were the closest to her. So, in the middle of my week at school, my sister came to pick me up so that we could go see our mother together.

Before traveling to Bouaké, my mother had gone through cataract surgery, and as sad as she was about her aunt, she wasn't allowed to cry. We all thought that this might be the reason she was feeling ill—because we thought it was extremely stressful to keep herself from crying when someone she loved very much has just died. When we arrived, even though my mother said she felt fine after she had passed out, my sister and I decided to take my mother back to my sister's house so that we could keep an eye on her.

While she was still in Bouaké visiting my sister, my mom was outdoors, sitting at the porch table and talking with one of the servants, when suddenly she stopped making sense. The servants called my sister at work, but in the meantime, I went directly to the house to see my mother. I also couldn't understand anything she said. I tried to help her back to her room, but she couldn't put her shoes on. We struggled even when I tried to help her.

When my sister got home, I told her about our mother's slurred speech. That's when my sister decided that we needed to get our mother to the hospital.

Honestly, I didn't know what was happening. I thought my mother was fine. With all of my 24 years of life experience, it didn't occur to me that she had perhaps suffered a stroke. But this was the doctor's explanation for her symptoms when we got my mother's test results back inside the hospital.

The doctor said their main goal was to get her stable. Every night, I slept on the floor or in a chair next to my mother's bed. I was a year and a half into law school, and I already began to see that caring for my mother in her current state was going to be a full-time job because of the abilities the stroke had taken from her. Even things as basic as eating and drinking were difficult for her at that point.

Mentally, I started to work on what it would look like to step away from my dreams of moving to the United States after getting my bachelor's degree—so that I could be with my mother. Maybe I could go to school part-time, but in my heart, I wanted to take care of her the same way she had taken care of me after the accident when I was hit by the ambulance.

After a week in the hospital, the doctors said that they had been able to get her stable, and we could take her back to my sister's home. When we arrived home, my mother suddenly became very weak. In the middle of the night, I took her back to the hospital. I remember the total sense of dread that went through my entire body. I was scared.

With my feet planted on the ground next to her hospital bed, I stayed and waited as the medical staff came in and out doing test after test. I didn't sleep at all that night. Feelings came and went away, surfacing like waves, as my mind warned me, *Your heart is slipping away, the most important person, the biggest love of your life.* I did everything I could to keep her alert while I stood there, my legs shaking from exhaustion and fear.

Seeing my mother in that state was one of the most difficult things I have ever had to face. And that was only the beginning of what would be the most intense moment of grief I've faced to this day—the fear that gripped me was real, and the reality of potential loss felt like more than I could manage.

When Grief Becomes Scarcity

The next morning, my mother was transported via ambulance to a bigger hospital for more tests. It was like we had gone back in time. There we were, in an ambulance together again. But this time, it was her, not me, fighting for her life while I watched on—feeling more hopeless than I ever had before.

After my mother got settled into a room, someone on the hospital staff came back with test results that my mother was anemic, which was probably responsible for her weakness. Like in many hospitals around the world, this hospital depended on family members to donate blood that could be used directly for their relatives. The nurse sent me to have blood drawn, but by the time I got back from giving blood, my mother was dying. I watched from the doorway as the woman I loved most in the entire world perished before my eyes.

The stroke had taken her.

I honestly don't remember a lot of details of what happened after she passed. That is something that my brain injury has stolen from me, like in other high-stress moments in my life. I do remember that my sister was out on location for her work. I don't remember what I said or did in response to such a huge loss in the following minutes and hours. I do know that even all of these years later, I still ask myself, *What if I had run quicker back to her hospital room? Would I have been able to say goodbye before she started on her journey to depart from this world?*

At the time, I was in shock. I felt numb. When I thought about my mother's death, not one tear escaped from my eyes. I had finally met a kind of scarcity that I felt I couldn't leverage—the scarcity of grief.

There will be moments in each of our lives when we are caught off guard. Some of these moments will redefine us. For me, my mother's death was one of those moments.

If you remember, after I was hit by the ambulance, I had to stay home so I was protected from the risks of the outside world. I was in a fragile state. My family didn't want me to get hurt and undo whatever the experimental surgery had done to save my life. But after my mother died, I didn't care about what would happen.

I wanted to take countless risks.

The idea that had motivated me to make good decisions—that I had already given my family too much drama after my accident to ever cause them trouble again—was gone the moment my mother died.

I partied and drank as I embraced the numbness brought to me by grief and pursued a lot of behaviors I had previously shunned in my personal pursuit of excellence.

Honestly, I lost my will to live. But simultaneously, part of me felt like I couldn't disappoint my sisters by giving up on school. They were also grieving after all. So, somehow I managed to earn my law degree.

Part of my risk-taking also involved having multiple girlfriends. At one point, a woman finally seemed to command my sole attention as I started to feel a connection with her. And as a result of our prolonged time together, she became pregnant. This news brought a fresh wave of grief because I thought, *My mother will never meet my children.*

Nine months later, the most amazing thing happened: My son was born. His birth changed everything in my life.

A Compelling Reason to Care

Learning to leverage relational scarcity was something I thought I had mastered. I did it in my middle school, in my high school, in my local community, and in law school. But the relationship I had with my son changed everything from the moment he came into the world.

One of the most important things my son has taught me is: Living for just yourself isn't enough. You also have to live for others.

Once my mother was gone, I lost my motivation to become truly excellent. I felt I was in a sort of functional despair, barely making it through each day, surrounded by the fog of grief. But when my son was born, I knew I needed to get my motivation back because I had someone extremely important to provide for.

Death has the ability to take something from us. It steals the joy the sound of our loved one's laughter can bring. It rips the knowledge we've stored inside their minds out of our lives forever. It takes confidence away that they had previously gifted us whenever we would meet. My mother's death taught me that the scarcity of grief carves a chunk out of our souls.

But my son's birth partially filled the large hole my mother's loss left in my life. It felt as if scarcity was saying to me, "Listen, I know you've been through something awful, but I'm giving you a new trajectory—it's time to get back to your plan."

That's the moment my desire to move to the US—to create a better path forward in life—was reborn. I didn't look forward to leaving my son, but I knew that I had to wake up from my functional despair (living my life through the fog of grief— and barely surviving). It was vital for me to relocate to a place where not everything reminded me of my mom.

I needed to use an external opportunity (which I shared about in chapter 1) to change my environment in order to get my life back on track. It was honestly the only way I could keep going.

You already know what my childhood was like: full of emotional, resource, and mindset scarcity. I never once felt like, *I have money to do something fun. What do I want to do with it?* And I wanted my son's life to be different. I wanted him to be able to choose something to spend *extra* money on during his childhood. Even though I am so thankful for everything scarcity has taught me and continues to teach me, back then, I wanted a different path for my son's life.

With my mindset returning to me piece by piece, and as I welcomed my son into the world, I prepared to leave. The US was waiting (through another miracle that grief gave me that I'll explain in the next chapter). It was through the loss of my mother and the gift of my son that I learned the scarcity of grief could only be overcome by relearning to appreciate life.

My son's arrival in my life diminished the pain I felt from losing my mother. You bring this little human being to earth, and it comes into the spaces of your mind that grief left empty and bleeding—and then, when that miracle of life begins to occupy your thoughts, you can see your options in a different light. It was through this opportunity that I saw a path that allowed me to confront the scarcity of grief—which I don't think is something you can really leverage until a lot of time has passed after that first moment when grief has come into your life.

Now, I want to walk you through how you too can confront the scarcity of grief by living for others, and how you can approach the difficult changes that life can bring, so that you understand how to move through those feelings.

Living for Yourself Isn't Enough

When I faced the scarcity of grief for the first time, I couldn't dig myself out of the hole I was in alone. Even though the motivation of keeping my sisters happy propelled me through that last year of law school, their love for me wasn't enough to break through the numbness I felt, still living on this Earth without my beloved mother.

But when my son was born, some light finally shone down into the hole I was in. My son's light propelled me to go far away from the things that reminded me of my mom (that I saw literally everywhere). My son became that someone else I was living for. And the first time he smiled at me, I was stunned to see the miracle before me: He had my mother's smile.

I don't want you to think that having a baby was some magical cure for my grief because it wasn't. Time also needed to pass. Some people describe grief as something you will carry with you forever. At first, it feels like a giant rock pressing you into the ground. Eventually though, it will shrink down, first to a suitcase you get tired of lugging around, and then to the size of a backpack that you can manage to carry. However, I don't believe we ever really set our grief down and move on entirely.

The first response many of us feel when we encounter grief is that we must isolate ourselves from others. But I can tell you that doesn't work. Why? Because living for just yourself isn't enough. That's why we all need to know how to RISE when we encounter this specific brand of scarcity.

Learn to RISE

When the scarcity of grief strikes, there is a framework you can use that I've developed based on my own experiences. I want you to remember that you can always RISE:

1. Realize what is going on around you.
2. Identify whose life you can make better.
3. Step into a posture of sacrifice.
4. Expect that hope will come back into your life over time.

Let's take a look at each letter in the RISE framework so that you know what to do when life gives you scarcity that feels too difficult to leverage.

Realize What Is Going on Around You

The most important thing to do when it feels like your world is falling apart is to acknowledge that you are going through something extremely difficult. Journal or record a voice memo on your phone or computer to explain to yourself that what you are experiencing is real, and your reactions are valid. Read or listen to that as many times as you need to for as many days, weeks, or months as it takes to realize and acknowledge your situation.

It is almost impossible to leverage mindset scarcity when you feel like, in contrast to what you've gone through, continuing to live with purpose isn't important. Grief will lie to you and say that without the person you lost, you are worthless and that there is no hope. This is the most concentrated form of mindset scarcity any of us will ever experience.

When you're able to tell yourself that it is okay to feel upset, angry, despondent, or discouraged because something big *has* happened to you, that's when you can start to leverage mindset scarcity because you are forcing your brain to acknowledge the truth of your situation. That is why *realize* is the first step in RISE—you have to realize what is truly going on before you can work through it.

Once I realized that staying in places that constantly reminded me of my mother made me feel even worse, that's when I could create a plan to allow me to acknowledge that I needed a change of scenery. Before that, I felt pretty helpless. But that's not where the RISE framework stops.

Identify Whose Life You Can Make Better

As you know, the birth of my son made it clear whose life I could make better if I got back to my plan to become someone important, like the men I had watched all those years before from the bridge.

When you're only thinking about yourself, it makes it difficult to make any moves forward. But when there is someone depending on your help, that is motivation unlike any other.

So for this step, identify and write down three people and one group that you know need your help. If you don't have one person in mind, then help a group. Volunteer at a place where they need people—just set yourself up to make a difference in the lives of others. When you are able to find people who need your help, that is when you can begin to build purpose in your life again. This is when you can live for someone else. If you don't have anyone to help, you need to find someone, or you won't be able to find light in the hole that grief can create inside of you.

Identifying who you're living your life for beyond yourself is the second step in RISE to help you work through hard things you will face.

Step Into a Posture of Sacrifice

Identifying who you can help isn't enough on its own to show you the reason why it's important to RISE. You have to take action in order to see results that will help you work through grief-based issues in your life.

You need a place where you can step into what I call a posture of sacrifice.

What are you willing to do for others—and actually follow through with? I promise you, if you aren't sacrificing for another person, then you won't be able to RISE. Why?

Sacrificial acts of love feed life back into our bodies and love back into our hearts, even when we feel empty.

For me, that meant getting serious about my plan to move to the US to build a better life for my son. This meant sacrificing seeing him in the short term because *of course* I wanted to be with my son. But I knew that to give him a different life than the one I had experienced, I needed to make a big change. Even if it meant leaving him for a period of time. So, that's what I did. Thankfully, my sacrifice would prove to be worth it.

While doing the first three steps in RISE will help you face the scarcity of grief, there's one more thing that I wish more people would talk about: how your feelings transform when you have distance from your grief.

Expect That Hope Will Come Back Into Your Life Over Time

Earlier, I shared that it wasn't just focusing on my son or moving away from the memories of my mother that allowed me to work through my grief: I also needed time. And you will too—to work through whatever hard thing comes into your life.

This is why you need to expect your feelings to change over time. Sometimes people will say, "You just need to hope things will get better." In this light, I feel that those people might never deal with their own grief. Sometimes, you can't muster the strength to hope that life will get better, and you must actively wait for hope to come back into your life.

And as you do the *E* in RISE, that is exactly what you're waiting for: *Expect* hope to come back. And I promise, dear reader, it will. But not if you try to rush into anything. Please, expect your feelings to change with time—which means you need to be patient with yourself and how you feel when you go through something hard.

Give Yourself Grace and Space

As you think about the final letter in RISE, I want to bring up one more point: Give yourself grace (love and understanding for you and your situation) when difficult things happen. This might mean pausing your dream or vision for a while so that you can readjust. And it's okay to do that.

This is a kind of starting over because when you go through something like losing a person who has helped shape who you are (like my mother), you need space to find who you are without that person. The same can be true about circumstances, like the loss of a job or experiencing something traumatic like a car accident.

You will need the space to discover who you are whenever you move through a change of circumstance, whether they are related to grieving over a lost loved one or not.

If you embrace the tools and give yourself the grace and space to RISE, that is how you can find light in any dark hole you are in. Even in the scarcity of grief, grace and space remind you that living for yourself isn't enough. And when you are ready to dream again, RISE will help you remember your vision for life (which we talked about in chapter 1).

Reset, Restart, Repeat

In this final part of the chapter, I want you to work through two exercises that are based on different parts of the RISE framework above.

Evaluating Your Circumstances

Identify a particularly difficult time in your life—maybe one where grief struck like it did for me with my mother's death. It could be one that you're going through right now, or something that happened in the past. With that event in mind, walk through the steps below and see where the exercise takes you. This way, you can see how you might have approached it to RISE so that the next time you experience a difficult moment, you'll know what to do.

The first step in the RISE framework—Realize what is going on around you—is vital. And within this step, you have a unique opportunity to get curious about how you can work through your difficult circumstances. Curiosity is part of realizing because it drives you to ask questions about what is really happening in your life. Nathan Gerbrandt argues that curiosity can help you be less judgemental of others, and I would add that it makes you less judgemental of yourself as well.[3]

With that event, past or present, in your mind, go through these five specific questions and answer them for the last loss or discouraging circumstance you faced.

1. What did I expect to happen during that time, and what happened instead?

2. What emotions did I experience when that occurred, and did I allow myself to thoroughly feel those emotions?

3. What part of that experience made me feel like I didn't have control—and what can I actually control as I work through this?

4. If I were talking to a friend I love who was going through this difficult thing and approaching them with curiosity and compassion instead of judgement, what would I say to them?

5. What is this hard situation showing me about what means the most to me in my life right now?

---

3   Nathan Gerbrandt, "The Power of Shifting Judgement to Curiosity," Crisis & Trauma Resource Institute, accessed March 24, 2025, https://ctrinstitute.com/blog/the-power-of-shifting-judgement-to-curiosity/.

Next, we're going to look at a different part of the RISE framework to help you respond to any opportunities that the scarcity of grief is bringing into your life.

Responding to Your Opportunities

In the *S* part of RISE, the focus is on stepping into a posture of sacrifice. Why? Because as we discussed, living for yourself isn't a compelling enough reason to help you keep your long-term vision. And while it is more than fine to pause your vision (giving yourself grace and space), it will be difficult to find hope again in life if you give up on your vision altogether.

As you step into the posture of sacrifice, I want to help you identify opportunities to do so.

First, research at least three ideas about how you can serve others. Then, ask the following questions for each opportunity to determine which one will best help you as you work through the RISE framework.

1. What skills do I have that will help the person or people related to this idea?

2. What skills can I develop along the way while I am helping this person or group of people?

3. As I step into the posture of sacrifice for this person or group of people, what qualities do I need that I already have?

4. What qualities do I need that I am missing and need to learn?

5. Which of the following categories will my helping this person or group of people allow me to explore:

leadership, asking others for help, working to become excellent, community building, or evaluating internal/external opportunities?

Based on the answers to those questions, you now have enough information to pick which person or group you want to enter a posture of sacrifice for. Nice work.

Grief is a brutal kind of scarcity that drains your emotions, steals the support you once had, and leaves you feeling a deep emptiness. It touches every part of your life, making it the hardest loss to carry. When it comes into your life, remember to be kind to yourself and take the time you need so that you can RISE.

In the next chapter, you are going to see that in the middle of big changes, you can also FLEX.

PART 2

WHEN *AGAIN* BECOMES A FRIEND

CHAPTER 6

The Brutality of Lonely Within

The things that happen in this life won't always make you feel like your next big opportunity is waiting just around the corner. If I'm being honest, I've learned that many times opportunity isn't waiting right there for you. You have to go out and find it. After my son was born and I found inspiration in wanting to provide for him, I wasn't sure what my next steps would be.

Even though I was still surrounded by friends and family in Côte d'Ivoire in a state where the scarcity of grief was a constant companion, I still felt alone. I want to tell you, dear reader, that feeling alone and *being* alone are two extremely different things, and you're going to see how in this chapter.

At this point in my story, with the loss of my mother, there were people around me who noticed I wasn't acting myself. That I had stopped working to help others. That I couldn't even function most days. Yes, I had that motivation I needed to start to break free of the numbness that encompassed me—but I still needed help.

So, my brothers and sisters created a plan.

The Gift Grief Gave Me—A Plane Ride to a New Life

Earlier I told you that a miracle had occurred in my life because of the scarcity of grief. But what I didn't tell you was that before my mother died, I had been rejected for a visa to go to the US ten times over the span of ten years. I remained determined to keep trying, and I thought that graduating from law school would make me an even better candidate to get accepted, but when the scarcity of grief came into my life, I lost my motivation to try. But after my son's birth, despite my numbness, I still cared about going to the US very much.

When my family saw my state after the loss of our mom, they decided to do something about it.

My brother, who had already been living in the US, offered to pay to sponsor me so that I could get a student visa. That also meant he would need to pay for my tuition for a year.

So, I packed my bags, said my goodbyes, and boarded the plane. At the same time, I couldn't believe that what was finally happening was real. Even after the plane landed in San Francisco, California, I thought I might still wake up and discover the entire trip had been a wild dream.

And when I realized it *wasn't* a dream, well, that's when things got even wilder for me.

Am I Still Myself When I'm Someplace Else?

Moving to the US was both everything I thought it would be and nothing I thought it would be. You see, the presence of scarcity must have had a plane ticket too. It followed me.

But once I had been removed from a familiar environment full of continuous reminders of my mother, that's when I remembered I could leverage scarcity. I had done it so many times before. However, I hadn't done it in the face of *such* an extreme change, one that included becoming part of a different culture using a different language.

What do I mean?

Sometimes in life, when you change circumstances, in order to fit in, you can be tempted to change who you are on the deepest levels. Maybe you try to minimize your accent or eat different foods. Maybe you keep all your hometown stories to yourself and try to divorce who you are now from the person you were growing up. I know that the pressure to fit in can be extreme. You witnessed that part of my story in every different place and school I went to. But remember, I was able to adapt because I knew who I was at my core. I knew I was *willing* to change things that were not part of the human I was at my core, that I was flexible with my ideas about *myself*.

When I moved to California, I realized something I hadn't really ever heard anyone else talk about: When you are willing to be flexible at your core—with your culture and your beliefs— you can adapt to new places or circumstances without feeling like you've lost yourself.

If your core is something that can be molded, you can bring that self with you into a new life, a new place, as you start again. As I moved ahead in my personal journey, the choices I made would give me hints as to who I was—at my core—along the way. In chapter 4, I shared with you about my carnival of character. It was through noticing myself taking action that I realized the kind of person I was—someone with a dynamic sense of integrity. There were also physical and mental difficulties I faced and still face today (because of my brain injury, loss of hearing, and the inability to know which side of my body is which without the scar on my right hand). This is why, at times, my writing may read differently—as I try to keep true to who I am and how I speak.

Who I am at my core is made up of things I cannot change. My integrity, my physical limitations, my birthplace of Côte d'Ivoire, and my faith in God. Those are the center of who I am. But I can interpret that core in different ways as I work through different situations. And that is exactly what I needed to do to succeed as an immigrant in general—but also specifically as an immigrant in the US.

It is possible to work through complex changes in your life, too, by interpreting your own core self through a lens that will help you as you work to transform your circumstances.

But in order to accomplish this, you have to believe in yourself, validate your feelings, and allow yourself time and space to work through shocks that may come along the way. Especially culture shock (which I'm going to define in a moment). So, let's take a look at my entry into the US, talk about my difficulty with culture shock, and learn what it meant for me to be flexible with my core self in practice. Are you ready?

Embracing the Blank Canvas—What Do I Want My Life to Look Like?

As I started exploring my new city of Oakland, California and thinking about the promise of school, even in the middle of my grief, I felt like I was slowly returning to my core self. The person I was before my mother's death. The man I had become, and the brave person who had used scarcity again and again in my life to carve the path I had dreamed of—standing on that bridge near my stepfather's house so long ago.

I thought, *Moving to the US gives me a blank canvas which now represents my life. What am I going to paint on it? What story will I see when I look back years from now at how the paint strokes came together?*

I knew that it was common for immigrants to come to the US and create entirely new stories for themselves. And I had heard those different stories from the immigrants who came before me. There were good stories, bad stories, medium stories, and stories that amazed and inspired me.

But all of the stories included one element that I knew I would be unable to escape: culture shock.

A Shocking Combination of Scarcity and Opportunity

As transportation and relocation has become easier with our ever-changing technology, allowing people to travel to and live in faraway places, there has been one observable emotion that many books have been written about and studies done to discover why it happens. I think that the main reason people are so curious about culture shock is that it's an experience that must be confronted and survived for every immigrant everywhere, all across the world.

Culture shock can be defined as feeling both surprised and stressed by new surroundings that don't match the way of life you were used to in your home country. And there are different stages that immigrants will experience in the observable and very real cycle of culture shock.

During the first stage, the recently relocated person will often experience joy and curiosity about their new environment and the people in it. This is why the unofficial name of this time is the "honeymoon phase."

The second stage, which is identified as the "crisis" part of this cycle, can create an attitude of disdain in immigrants for their new host culture. This might look like being resistant to eating food from other cultures, feeling upset when cultural practices differ in various communities, or suffering from homesickness in a way that creates bitterness for the people around them who haven't chosen to leave their home country. These feelings can even mimic symptoms of a disease, leading to observable results like continuous hand washing, fear of physical contact with others, outbursts of anger, and brain fog.[4]

---

4 Kali A. Demes and Nicolas Geeraert, "The Highs and Lows of a Cultural Transition: A Longitudinal Analysis of Sojourner Stress and Adaptation Across 50 Countries," *Journal of Personality and Social Psychology*, 109, no. 2 (2015): 316–337. https://doi.org/10.1037/pspp0000046.

When I left Côte d'Ivoire, I knew that I needed a fresh start. At the same time, I also knew that I didn't have the money to get back home if I needed to—because it was unlikely I would ever be able to afford a plane ticket back, which meant I might never see my son, my family, or my friends from my home country ever again.

That is a reality that many immigrants face. They scrape and save for years or decades to leave their home countries, yet they don't know if they will ever be able to return. And this contributes to the feelings of culture shock.

The more I thought about my own huge transition to the US after the fact, and especially as I was working on this book, the more I realized that culture shock is a unique combination of the three different types of scarcity.

First, you have resource scarcity. You managed to bring together a lot of resources just to get to the place where you want to go. There are visa fees, plane tickets, and—if you're lucky—some moving expenses. Lucky because many of us have moved to other countries with nothing more than a backpack or small suitcase with a few clothes inside. And once your flight lands, you have to figure out how to pay for basic things to live: food, a place to stay, the thing you promised the country you were going there to do (which, in my case, was study in university for a master's degree—and I knew that was going to cost a lot).

Then, you have some of the most intense emotional scarcity you can imagine. And it's not just that you have left everything and everyone you know and love and you're totally alone. If you have a language barrier, that means you can't even talk to strangers—and that is a whole new level of being alone. That was an emotional scarcity that I hadn't experienced before. Because even after my accident when I spent most days alone with my friends the ants, I still saw my family when they came home at the end of each day. In the US, I could be alone for hours, days, or even weeks without anyone saying a single word to me.

And on the off chance that someone did talk to me, I couldn't understand them because they spoke English and I spoke French. The language barrier was something I knew I needed to adapt for right away.

At the same time, both resource and emotional scarcity can contribute to increased mindset scarcity, especially when you consider how alert your brain is to the intense differences all around you in your new location.

Plus, even though I was trying to run from the scarcity of grief, my companion of scarcity also played a huge role in the culture shock I felt. Whenever you lose something familiar to you—a person, a place, a way of living—grief comes in. It's an unavoidable presence in your life at that point.

And by moving and starting over, I had lost everything. My access to my son. My relationships with my friends and family. My reputation as a remarkable student and community member. I also lost the standard knowledge of what was expected of me from others—because when you go to a new culture, you can't assume you know what the people around you will anticipate from you.

Whatever scarcity I had experienced up until that point in my life had been intense, but the scarcity that came along with culture shock was wild to me. The amount of scarcity wrapped up in this one idea felt completely overwhelming.

At the same time, I saw an intense opportunity before me as I looked around at my new world—an external opportunity shaped by a totally new environment that held possibilities that would have never been available to me back home.

This is when I realized my life in this new country *really was* a blank canvas—it didn't just feel like one—and I could take the same approaches to leverage scarcity that I had already used my entire life. I could choose which picture I wanted to paint. And I could move through culture shock as long as I was flexible with my core self.

Yes, at my core I was an African man with integrity and physical limitations, but I could still exist as myself in a new place by being open to what the different people with their varying cultures could teach me.

That doesn't mean my new adventure was easy. Right away, I knew that my first priority would have to be gathering more resources if I wanted to stay in the US. And after that, before I got too dejected, I needed to address my loneliness.

Finding a Sort of Belonging in Work

Even though my brother had sponsored me and allowed me to stay in a room in his apartment, he was busy working and taking care of his children. And that meant that I was constantly alone.

My brother had done a huge favor for me by sponsoring my visa, and I appreciated that so much. But realistically, he couldn't keep paying for my tuition. So when he told me I needed to find a way to make money to pay for my school, I wasn't surprised. But I also didn't know what to do because I didn't have a visa that allowed me to work—or at least do the kind of work that directly supported my future goals of becoming successful. Let me explain.

I remember I got an interview at a chain restaurant. But as soon as the interview started, the kind woman who interviewed me asked for my work visa. When I told her I didn't have one, she said she was sorry she couldn't hire me, but I could still find work in specific places based on the visa I *did* have.

From what the woman shared, I had two choices before me. I could either find a super low-paying job on campus at UC Berkeley where I was studying English at their language school. Or, I could take a job that no one else wanted and get paid under the table. With her advice in mind, I made a plan.

At this point in my stay, I had started walking the city at all hours, hoping I would run into strangers who would be willing to talk to me. My English was getting better, and one day I met a kind man in the park who told me he had a friend who needed help at a club. One of those late-night places where people go to forget their cares, drink, and dance the night away.

I thanked the man and set up an appointment with his friend. Since it was the only job I could get at the time, I took the position which included things like using the commercial dishwashing machine, cleaning the bathrooms, and mopping the floor at the club. This meant that I worked into the early morning hours—every single night. And sometimes, I still didn't have the money to take the bus or the train home, so I would stay in the city until my next shift started.

Back home in Abidjan, I had been one of the young people *enjoying* my time with other students. I wasn't one of the people who visited the night clubs, because I enjoyed more intellectually focused hangouts. But I had been the one enjoying time with friends. In Oakland, California, I was the one cleaning up everyone's vomit while the young people around me had fun. This contrast I felt gave me the sense that I had taken a step back in life. I still remember that for the first week I worked at the club, I cried every night.

But at least I was creating relationships with the other workers, even if they spoke Spanish and I spoke mostly French. When I was at the club, I was never alone. Still, though, I can't say I wasn't still lonely.

Even during this difficult season, I was determined to leverage scarcity whenever and wherever I could, so each day I would work through the mindset scarcity I faced by thinking to myself, *You have to make every day count. You are capable of moving through this situation.*

Little did I know that God was about to step into my life in a powerful way to give me not only better resources but also fellowship and emotional support.

Making Friends in the House of God

You remember, dear reader, that when I was in middle school, one of the things I did every day was read the Bible. The words on those pages kept me company, along with the ants, on long days when I had to sit alone and do nothing. When I got to California, I was determined not to let my faith dissolve. So I would still go to the church in my neighborhood whenever I could—which wasn't often because of the demanding hours of my job.

One day, I went into the church office to pay my tithes. Even though I wasn't getting paid a lot and I had already had to transfer to a cheaper language school, I still wanted to make sure to give God part of what I had.

The secretary in the office, who I learned was named Ms. Jackie, looked up at me and said, "Why haven't I seen you around?"

I explained about my job at the club and how I worked the night shift, and sometimes that meant I couldn't make it back to our neighborhood on Sunday to attend church. She looked at me and then suddenly said, "I think I can help, but first, I know someone you should meet."

She introduced me to the pastor and a few other people at the church, and they became my new community. At the same time, Ms. Jackie told me that I could work for her and her husband at their group home for disabled children in foster care.

That was when mopping up vomit became a thing of the past, and I transitioned into a night shift job at the group home. Due to the fact I no longer had to make a commute to work, I had more free time, and I was able to use my community skills for the good of the church by volunteering to help with different tasks and programs. For example, I asked the pastor if he would be okay with me starting a youth group for the community, and he said yes. Within just a few months, we had created a safe space for the teens who lived around us, helping them to grow and thrive as they interacted with the loving members of our church.

And it was through that youth group that I would meet a very special person in my life—the woman who I would marry, Michelle (who I'll talk more about in the next chapter). There was also another special person I met during this season of my life that changed my personal and professional mission forever. It's time for you to meet Paul.

A Loneliness That Wasn't Chosen

Working in my new position in the group home, I experienced the biggest culture shock of my life. You see, in Côte d'Ivoire, we don't have group homes for children like the ones that exist in the United States. There are different reasons for this, but the one that I couldn't help but think of over and over again is that I didn't know anyone in my country who would abandon a child who had a disability. Because even if the child's parents couldn't take care of them, someone from the community would have stepped in to bring that child into their own family.

To me, the idea that a child would literally have no one was unimaginable.

When I first met Paul, one of the boys at the home, I lost sleep over his personal situation. He spent all his time alone in his bedroom. I did my best to brighten his life each time I saw him, with a smile, some conversation, and simple gestures to show him that I cared. I thought, *Well, if I can't take care of my mother since she's no longer here, I can at least take care of these children, like Paul, in a way that honors her memory.* That approach helped me take a step forward in healing.

But then, I worked my first Christmas at the group home.

Every other child was able to go visit family in some manner, except for Paul. The other children stayed with grandparents, aunt, uncles, and sometimes were even allowed to stay temporarily with parents who promised case workers that they would be on their best behavior. But no one came for Paul. And he spent the entire holiday break with me and the other group home employees as we took care of him during our corresponding shifts.

Each night, once I thought Paul was asleep, I went into my room and cried. My heart and my culture told me, "This isn't right! That a boy is left without any friends or family during what is supposed to be the happiest season of the year." When I had dreamed of moving to the US, I never imagined that such a tangible sadness would meet me there in the form of a teenage boy.

I thought about my own life. I had chosen to move to the US, to a new place. I knew I would be alone. Before I met my church brothers and sisters (as Christians we believe we are all children of God and therefore brothers and sisters), I had been in a state of brutal loneliness within. But that was a conscious decision I made as an adult. I came knowing I would be alone because I knew my brother was busy with his own family.

Paul had not chosen to be alone, and he was a child. As I thought back to all of the ways scarcity had been a presence in my life, I couldn't help but think of how much more scarcity Paul had to face every moment of his life.

By New Year's Eve, I couldn't take it anymore. So, I made a plan to take Paul to watch the ball drop in the city center in Oakland (which was a mini version of what they did in New York City). He didn't talk much, but when we got there, I could see in his eyes that in that giant crowd, Paul no longer felt alone. Paul's moment of community only lasted for about an hour, but it would go on to change my entire life (which you're going to see in later chapters).

When I looked at Paul's situation, and everything that had happened in my life, that's when I finally started putting some brush strokes on the blank canvas that began to tell the story of my life in the US.

I didn't know it at the time, but the way Paul allowed me to help him filled that part of my heart that had promised to take care of my mother—since, as you know, I never had an opportunity to fulfill that promise. At the same time, my work at the group home was about to come to a stop.

The Gardener and the Aide

Just before I got married, something happened at the group home. Though I loved working with the kids there, especially Paul, Ms. Jackie let me know she had made a mistake when they onboarded me as an employee. She hadn't realized that I didn't have a work visa. I had thought that since I was on a student visa and we did educational activities, it would allow me to work there. But I guess I had been wrong. Ms. Jackie told me I couldn't work at the group home anymore. My heart was broken, but I understood.

After letting me go from the group home, Ms. Jackie introduced me to Ms. Fisher, a woman at our church who owned a gardening business.

Ms. Fisher told me that she couldn't guarantee to pay me because I didn't have a work visa, but she said if I helped, they would give me whatever they could. And because, if you remember, I had worked hard to build relationships with the rural kids back in middle school, and they had shown me exactly what to do when we were working outside together, I had all the skills I needed to help Ms. Fisher with her work.

After I got married, Ms. Fisher realized I needed a better job with benefits and started to search with me to find such a job. I needed to find something that allowed me to keep balancing my studies with work while I continued to pay for my own tuition for the language school. At that point, I had taken the exams that proved I was fluent in English and allowed me to enroll in a normal university in the US.

I also worked various odd jobs here and there to bring in more of the income that we needed, including working at a restaurant. I was willing to do whatever it took and to be flexible with my positions, even if sometimes the work felt like I was taking a step backward. For all of those moments of feeling like I was going in the wrong direction, I reminded myself that if I had to take two steps forward and one step back to live my dream, that was okay. And that those steps backward were only temporary.

Because I was studying to be able to speak fluently in English, and I had been able to get a green card (also known as permanent resident card) through my marriage to my wife who was a US citizen, I knew that new jobs would be open to me. And I made a plan to further my teaching career. But before I could get there, I needed to heal the other half of my heart—the half that was quietly and secretly still swollen from the grief of my mother even after the birth of my son. And that was going to take another miracle.

At the same time, with my student visa, I had worked as a teacher's aide during the day when I didn't have classes. I specialized in classrooms helping the students who had special needs and were all in wheelchairs due to severe physical disabilities. This ended up being a huge blessing in my life because it allowed me to do what I had wanted to do in taking care of my mother during her paralysis after her stroke. I wished that I had been able to take her home and get her settled in her new normal, which I knew would include a wheelchair. But she hadn't lived, so my plan hadn't become a reality.

As an aide to the children at school, I was able to live out that internal promise I had made to my mother by caring for the students who needed my help. But I still needed a second job to support my wife Michelle and me.

Before we get to the next part of the story, I want to share the framework that this part of my life helped me create to navigate even the most soul-shaking situations I faced in a foreign country: the ability to be flexible with my core self.

The FLEX Framework

Throughout this chapter, you saw how I used flexibility during the loneliest time of my life. Looking back, I can see that it was being flexible with myself that allowed me to work to make progress toward my goals and dreams. This gave me an advantage that helped me manage the loneliness I felt.

When I arrived in the US, managing my loneliness began with solo walks in Oakland. Then I worked hard to learn English so that I could talk to people and went to parks and public places where I could interact with others. Then I applied for that first restaurant job only to have my hopes crushed and ended up working brutal night shifts at the club as the only member of the clean-up crew. Finally, I was able to build a community for myself at the church. And I got a job at the group home where I met Paul. Through church, we created a place for our community that the teens around us could get involved with. Next, I was able to work with Ms. Fisher in her gardening business. I met my wife, Michelle. And then I worked part time as a teacher's aide. All of these things happened in a short time frame, and some happened at the same time.

During this season, I learned that part of flexibility is being willing to keep going—even if that means doing some things that are outside of your comfort zone.

I was still the same person, but I wasn't limited by my own culture or my own personal experiences. Being flexible with my core self meant that I was willing to walk through things I hadn't been through before if it would help me adjust and learn.

So now, I want to help you understand what being flexible with your core self looks like so that you too can make it through even the most difficult moments of your life. Because scarcity is a character and has a presence, at some point, we must confront it and learn to manage it.

To help you navigate changes that can cause literal shock (like culture shock or the scarcity of grief), I'm going to introduce the FLEX framework. It will help you evaluate your circumstances in a particular order so that you can stay flexible by leveraging the three types of scarcity—emotional, resource, and mindset scarcity—when you face life-changing situations.

When you are in a situation where you have to confront all of the beliefs you hold about the world and yourself, make sure to FLEX:

1. Focus on self-awareness.
2. Listen to and evaluate your emotions.
3. Evaluate the level of change you're experiencing.
4. eXpand your mind with grace and intention.

Now we're going to break each of these ideas down.

Focus on Self-Awareness

Through the experiences I shared in this chapter, I was forced to look at all three different types of scarcity. But when it came to doing check-ins with myself, I was forced to think about emotional and mindset scarcity because they posed the greatest risks to my dreams. Every day, I needed to work through mental questions as I evaluated how I was going to get closer to completing my goals. That helped me become aware of what I was choosing for myself.

Here are the questions you can use to become more self-aware during huge life transitions:

- What is the vision I have for my future self?
- How do the plans I have today help me get closer to that vision?
- Where do I feel resistance between who I am and what I'm asking myself to do as I work toward my goals?
- How can I continue to honor who I am in the middle of these difficult goals?

When I was cleaning vomit in the club, there were many times when I thought, *Is this job really in line with who I am?* That was an uncomfortable job for me to do. But when I took a step back and answered the questions above, the money I got paid from working at the club helped me pay for my language school, which I was going through to help set me up to work well in the US. I had to learn English. Period.

Using a mop and bucket as my primary work tools wasn't the biggest boost for my pride, but it was still aligned with my vision because it brought me closer to my goals. I did need to be aware of how that job made me feel and why I was willing to do it to keep going.

You can also use these questions to help *you* be aware of *your* feelings. This will help you confront a big change and understand how the work associated with it can move you closer to where you want to go. In the next step, we'll talk about what to do with the feelings you have after you've worked to be more self-aware.

Listen to and Evaluate Your Emotions

In order to understand why you're feeling the way you do in the midst of big changes, here are the steps you can work through.

- *Name the feeling.* Are you experiencing resentment, hope, anxiety, joy, or stress? Write that feeling down in a journal or on your phone.

- *Remind yourself that what you are feeling is normal.* It is okay to feel however you are feeling. Big changes in life bring up all sorts of emotions.

- *Encourage yourself.* Ask yourself what you would say to a friend feeling the same way as you and then give yourself that same empathy and compassion.

When I experienced culture shock as a result of meeting Paul and witnessing his situation, I cried a lot. I felt extreme sorrow because of what he was going through. That wasn't something I had ever seen before: a child who was forced to be alone.

Over time, I was able to remind myself that what I was feeling made sense, and I encouraged myself to do what I could for Paul. At the same time I had to remember that I couldn't actually rescue Paul from his situation—but I could let my feelings about his circumstances shape the choices I would make in the future.

After you've done this step, the next focus is on understanding how much change you're going through because the amount of change matters.

Evaluate the Level of Change

Different levels of change will create different amounts of stress. But more change can also provide bigger opportunities (like we saw in chapter 1). Here, we are going to look at change through the lens of the three different types of scarcity.

As you work through each section below, think about the level of change each answer brings out.

Emotional Scarcity & Change

Ask and answer the following questions to determine your level of change:

- Will I need to let go of certain beliefs about myself, the world, and my role in the world because of the level of change I'm going through?
- Will I experience pain or excitement, or both?
- What can I do with these feelings? (Look up at the previous section for help navigating this question.)

Resource Scarcity & Change

Ask and answer the following questions to continue to determine your level of change:

- Which resources am I losing in this new situation?
- Which resources am I gaining because of this change?

- What new support systems will I need to develop to address this amount of change? (You can go to the "Reset, Restart, Repeat" section of chapter 1 for help with this question.)

Mindset Scarcity & Change

This is probably the most difficult factor of the three we're discussing when it comes to big change—mindset scarcity. Why? Because your brain will resist anything it doesn't already know, so big changes can put your brain into fight or flight mode.[5] In order to work through the stresses associated with big change, you can ask these questions to help your brain see the changes in a nonthreatening light:

- Is what I'm going through challenging my old beliefs, ideas, and definitions of success?

- How can I approach new ideas in a flexible way to see the opportunities and possibilities in them to calm my mind?

- What updated mindsets do I need to help me through this season of change?

As you look through your answers in the three categories, I suggest you rate whether a change is small, medium, or large so that you know how much time and energy to dedicate to working through each one. Remember, not all changes are equal. When you can look at how big a change is, you can set realistic expectations on how you can deal with each change in a more effective way.

---

5 Howard E. LeWine, ed., "Understanding the Stress Response," Harvard Health Publishing, April 3, 2024, https://www.health.harvard.edu/staying-healthy/ understanding-the-stress-response.

Now, let's look at the final step in the FLEX framework.

eXpand With Grace and Intention

At this point, you've already looked at the practical thoughts and choices you can make to adjust during your season of change through the *F*, *L*, and *E* of the FLEX framework. Next, look at how the big changes of life affect you with compassion and vision for your future self by thinking about how you can expand:

- **Give yourself permission to expand.** Out loud, say this to yourself, "I allow myself to grow without abandoning my core self—whom I have chosen to be as I have leveraged scarcity in my life."

- **Create small wins.** Prove to yourself that you are making progress in this phase of intense change. Choose one small action each day to help you FLEX toward the next goal you have as you support your life's vision.

- **Find the ways change is making you better.** Ask and answer the following questions:
  - » What is one thing I'm doing well in how I'm adapting? How does this make me proud of myself?
  - » What is the compass that I bring along with me from before I made this change that shows me where to go? How is showing up for myself with that compass proving that I can trust myself with change?

As I worked in different places, switched to a more affordable language school, and found community and meaning at work and at church, I was able to navigate the big change I had experienced. This helped me prove to myself that I could still leverage scarcity and find opportunities in a season of profound change—even when I had never experienced the loneliness I felt in the US before.

Because I was able to remind myself of my vision so that I could FLEX during this time, what could have been an extremely damaging experience helped prepare me for the next phase of life: learning to be a husband and an in-person father. That's what is coming next in my story. But first, I want to give you an opportunity to use the FLEX framework yourself.

Reset, Restart, Repeat

In your life, you *will* encounter big changes. Maybe you won't move to a different country or culture, but you will still go through different phases of life as you age and learn more about the world around you—and your place in it. For this exercise, I want you to give yourself permission to answer the following questions with complete honesty. Then, think about what the answers mean and how you can use the information you find here to help yourself adapt to the big changes coming your way.

Grab a pen and paper or your phone or laptop so that you can record your answers to the following questions:

1. What part of my core self do I want to protect and bring with me through this change? (For me, I wanted to keep my dedication to helping others like Paul, in an effort to honor the life of my mother.)

2. What emotion feels like it is the loudest right now— and what is the emotion asking me to do? (My biggest

emotion during my move to the US was loneliness, not just because of the grief I experienced when I lost my mother, but because of the isolation I felt as I learned how to exist in a new country and culture.)

3. If I take a step back and look at my entire situation, where do I feel like I'm being stretched most—in my emotions, in my resources, or in my mindset? (While I was lacking resources once I moved to the US, the biggest types of scarcity I struggled with on a daily basis were emotional and mindset related.)

4. What is one belief or action I can choose today that honors both who I am and who I'm becoming? (When I kept thinking back to my core self during this intense season of change, I knew that I wanted to grow my abilities through school while giving myself chances to make the lives of other people better.)

As you go through different transformations in life—whether because of a move, a moment of loss, or an opportunity you can't pass up—remember that you can be flexible without losing yourself. Your core self. And what you learn along the way is wisdom you can use to work toward your vision.

CHAPTER 7

Getting Brave Again and Again

In the last chapter, you met Paul, a person who would go on to shape my life in an intense way. But someone you didn't officially meet was my wife, Michelle. In this chapter, I want to finally introduce you to the woman who would change my life in profound ways through her kindness and support.

That means we need to rewind a bit, to before Paul and to before the group home, to a place in my story where even though things didn't exactly go according to plan, I learned how to be brave—even in the face of difficulties that no longer just had to do with me, but were affecting my family.

I want to let you know from the start that my story with Michelle doesn't have a typical fairy tale ending. Marriage is difficult, and you're going to see that in the next few chapters. Our journey brought along all sorts of scarcity for Michelle and me. At the same time, it also brought unique moments of triumph, love, and wisdom.

Which is exactly what I want to talk about in this chapter: the fact that some lessons can be best learned when roadblocks come into the picture. One of the most helpful ideas I've learned in my life is that roadblocks create opportunities. How? By forcing us to be more creative with the types of steps we take to live out each of our unique visions. Because when we are willing to trudge along on a path less traveled, that is when we can blaze our own trails that lead to the lives we want to live.

Starting Over Again—With Michelle

One of the biggest challenges I have faced in my life was living up to who I wanted to be as a husband. And even now, as a co-parent and friend, I work to make sure I am there for Michelle to support and cheer her on in every way I can. But before I get into all that in later chapters, I want to start at the beginning of our relationship.

In the last chapter, you will remember that one of the most amazing things that happened once I moved to the US was that I got involved at a church in Oakland. The people there gave me friendship, fellowship, and a chance to invest in the local community.

One day, I was there for a youth group event, and I wandered into the kitchen with a growling stomach.

Just then, a woman walked in and said, "Who are you?"

"I'm Max. I help with the youth group," I said.

"I'm Michelle. I work in the church's preschool," she said. "What are you doing in here?"

"I'm hungry," I said. My stomach growled to audibly agree with my words.

"Do you want me to make you something?" she asked.

"That would be amazing," I said. "Thank you."

Right away, I thought about how unique she looked. Her red hair and medium skin created a combination I hadn't seen before, and I asked her whether she was Mexican or Latina.

She said, "No, I'm Black."

I said, "From where Black?" (I thought about the Black people I had been surrounded by in Africa, and she didn't look like any of them.)

She laughed and then said, "From here Black."

As she prepared something for me to eat, we talked back and forth the entire time. I realized that I didn't want our conversation to end, so I asked her out on a date. She said yes, and that's when I found someone who dreamed of the future with me—of what we could be together.

I remember the first time I gave her a gift, I saved up for weeks to be able to buy her a fancy handbag. When she opened it she said, "Wow! This is amazing. And I know it's just the first of many gifts we will be able to give each other." While those were still early days in our relationship, the fact that she believed in my future success meant so much to me. And that belief pushed me further than I had pushed before. With her by my side, I felt a new sense of bravery that I hadn't before.

Even with all of the scarcity I had faced and leveraged, with Michelle in my life, I could face scarcity with more determination than I had managed before. At least, that's how I felt at first.

Within six months, we were married. It was fast, but I knew and she knew that we wanted to take the next steps into our future together. At the time, I was still working as a gardener and going to school.

In the early days of our marriage, we lived with Michelle's grandmother, who was an extremely generous and kind woman. As the two of them took care of me and gave me unconditional love, I felt another layer of healing take place in what had been an open, persistent wound after my mother had died. Having these two women think about my wants and needs reminded me of how my mother had loved and cared for me after my accident with the ambulance. But there was a deeper level of connection with Michelle, as she awakened my dreams on a new level again and again.

My beautiful and amazing wife would drive me around glamorous neighborhoods and point out different houses saying, "One day, that's the place we're going to rent." It reminded me of all those days I spent on the bridge dreaming of what I wanted my future to be.

At the same time, I have to admit I felt restless. While Michelle's grandmother provided a place for us to live when we first got married, I didn't want to depend solely on her generosity. I had seen some people back in Côte d'Ivoire who were always trying to get money from others, and I had always vowed to be an addition to the people in my life, not just someone content to use another person's resources. So, while I worked and was still an active student, I found a two-bedroom apartment for Michelle and me to move into.

I know my work experience list seems long and ever-changing as the winds of a tornado at this point, but there was also one more job I was working at the same time. Ms. Jackie had introduced me to someone who gave me yet another job as the program manager of an after-school care enrichment curriculum with activities available to students at a public school in that area.

As much as Michelle's grandmother wanted to help us financially, I knew that I needed to provide for my family myself. And that became an option once I became the after-school program manager. Plus, I had faced resource scarcity before, and I knew that to leverage it, I needed a concrete plan. So, when I wasn't gardening, working as an aide, managing the after-school program, or at school as a student myself, I studied like night and day to take the CBEST, the test for a certification I needed to become a substitute teacher.

I had already figured out how many days I would need to work as a substitute per school year to be able to afford the life I wanted to build for my small family—Michelle and me.

Substitute Triumphs and Troubles

One day while I was with the students at the after-school program, I got a phone call from Michelle. The fact she was calling me before I got home set off kind of an alarm because she didn't usually call while I was working. When I went to the office phone, her voice came through.

"You have an envelope here from the government. Should I open it?"

"Yes," I said, knowing it must be the results of my CBEST test. Whether or not I passed, it was time for me to be brave and find out how I had done.

"Okay," she said.

I could hear the paper tearing. The breath caught in my chest as I waited for the answer that paper held.

"You passed!" Michelle yelled through the phone. "You did it, Max!"

Even though I had used the intense study system I had learned from my cousin back in middle school, I was still sort of shocked. When I was taking classes and studying for the CBEST, they told us that most people who take it fail. They gave us some intimidating numbers to back up that claim, saying that out of 1,000 test takers, only 200 usually passed.

But on that day, I found I was one of the 200. I was part of the 20% that had succeeded. And that meant I could finally work as a substitute teacher. And specifically because of my background, I was able to be a substitute who worked with special needs students.

Honestly, that was one of the best days in my life, knowing that I had made my goal into reality. Especially when I thought about how many of the people who had taken the test hadn't passed.

Once again, I had been able to leverage an external opportunity by participating in the educational requirements the government had recommended for me to use to be able to pass that test. But, as always, scarcity followed me into the situation—ready with surprises I couldn't anticipate.

Even though I was excited to be a substitute teacher, I was up against both resource and emotional scarcity in that I didn't know what I didn't know. The resource scarcity had to do with the sporadic nature of my pay. I hadn't considered the problem that would arise in summer when there were no classes to substitute teach for. The emotional scarcity came into play because I didn't know which age group I would work best with, and until I figured that out, I had to test myself with kids of all different ages, which was stressful. Some of the groups were so loud, the noise wore on me because of my hearing difficulties. Plus, I was physically exhausted.

As it turned out, I wasn't the best with the smaller kids. Looking back, it makes sense that I wasn't exactly suited to work well with them. My hearing loss made it so that I was less effective in their collective din of noise. Plus, I didn't know how to discipline them when they wouldn't listen. I also didn't want to startle them with my deep voice if I was stern. They called me "Max," instead of "Mr. Max," and at first I didn't realize that was a respect issue.

After working my way through each age group, I learned that I loved working with the high school students best. They were at this amazing phase of life where they were figuring out who they were and could contribute their own ideas. Plus, they were generally quieter than the younger kids.

I also realized that with school and my new work as a substitute, I wouldn't be able to stay at the after-school program as the manager. I had already stopped working as a gardener before I started subbing because I needed to focus more on teaching and my own course work.

Leaving my other jobs meant I had to make sure I was subbing enough days to cover what we needed to pay rent for our apartment. At the same time, Michelle had become pregnant, and we were planning to welcome our first child. This time, I would actually get to be a part of the child's day-to-day life, which I hadn't been able to do with my son at that point in my life (the son I left back home in Côte d'Ivoire so that I could build a better life for all of us), and building a better life was important to me.

Michelle and I had originally chosen an apartment on the other side of Oakland, in Richmond, which was more affordable than where her grandmother lived. And for a while, we were making it. Paying rent, able to afford food. Scarcity had taken a brief vacation, or so it seemed. But then, summer came.

Today, in many states in the US, school districts spread paychecks for their teachers over the entire 12 months of a year. My first year as a substitute, in Northern California, that wasn't the case.

And it wasn't exactly that summer had caught me by surprise. I had heard the school staff talking about their summer-time jobs. But I had been so busy working and going to school that June had snuck up on me.

All of these circumstances created a need for me to do better and provide more, especially when my daughter came into the world (which happened around this time, but that I'm going to talk more about in the next chapter).

I knew there were still opportunities out there, and all I had to do was find them. But, of course, it wasn't going to be easy. And the path I found to provide more made me confront who I was yet again, just like when I had said no to the school president who wanted me to steal half of the students' money.

How Can They Even Understand You?

I did what I had learned to do before: I used the external opportunities based on my relationships with other people to find a solution. Thankfully, the principal at the school where I had worked at the after-school program was a friend of Michelle's aunt. And when I told her I was looking for something during the summer break, she helped me get a job at a tutoring center—a place where parents could bring their kids for additional teaching and academic support.

There, I was tasked with providing enrichment for the students in the subjects of English and Math. At the tutoring center, there were constant reminders that I wasn't like everyone else. Mindset scarcity was there, tempting me to think of myself as strange or incapable. And even though I had leveraged it so many times, it was still difficult for me to adjust to the constant complaints I heard about things I just couldn't change. The most difficult thing to face each day was that some of my fellow teachers kept saying things like, "I don't know how the kids can even understand you with your thick accent."

I had worked *so* hard to master English, and it seemed that even those efforts weren't enough. There was no changing my accent, and honestly, I didn't want to try to change it. The way I spoke was a part of who I was. In each roll of the tongue and flourish of sound, my past and present combined to show the world what I was made of. And I was proud of everything I had survived. I was also thankful to God for who He made me to be, and I didn't want to try to hide that. But my resolve to be myself and embrace my unique voice and accent was about to be tested.

One warm day, which prompted me to make sure all of our classroom windows were open, I was working with a group of kids on an exit test (this exam would give them final scores to compare with their entrance scores). Part of the test required me to read them a paragraph so that they could respond to it. So I picked up the page and started to read the words out loud. There were a bunch of students outside getting ready to leave, and one of them came over to the window to listen to me speak. Then another. Then another.

Suddenly, there were more students crowded around the outside of my classroom than there were students inside my classroom. Next, some of the parents joined the students to see what they were doing outside the classroom.

I was only halfway through the paragraph when I realized the intimidating number of students and parents outside were all there because of the way I sounded reading the text. They were there to listen to my accent. The same accent other teachers had told me made it difficult for them to understand what I was saying.

In that moment, I had two choices. I could stop and make one of the students read the prompt to remove attention from me. Or, I could keep going until the end and allow these uninvited guests to scrutinize my pronunciation of each and every word. And as I looked out the window, I saw some faces filled with contempt and others with curiosity. In my heart, I knew that I couldn't let those who had visible contempt for my voice keep me from serving my students. So, I decided to fight—again and again.

Inside my mind, a war was waging. I knew what I wanted the outcome to be. But mindset scarcity was hitting hard, reminding me of all my deficiencies: that I was a foreigner who didn't have full command of the English language, that I had a traumatic brain injury and stress would often cause me to lose my words (and forget what I was trying to say), and that despite all of my struggling and hard work it was still difficult to cover the living costs for me and wife (who was also working hard at the church's preschool).

There was a voice inside that screamed for me to stop. To quit. To hand the page of text off to someone else. But there was also a confident voice that said, *With all you have been through, with all you have done to not just to survive but to thrive, you are going to get through this moment.*

When I finished reading, the students in my room looked up at me with smiles on their faces, ready to get to work. And the people who had been outside dispersed. The whole event probably took five to ten minutes, but those minutes shaped my life as a teacher. I had proven to myself that I could make it through the peering eyes of judgement if it meant serving my students. And the confidence I built in those few minutes propelled me forward through the rest of my teaching career and into my ultimate career as the CEO of A Bright Future, Inc.

One of the seeds planted during my time at the tutoring center was that we taught the students math and English, but it didn't seem like anyone anywhere was working with these kids on practical life skills. Things I had learned from my adventures in the neighborhood back home and from my family, the uncles and the aunties. I knew that needed to change and that I wanted to be a part of making it happen—at least for the students I was able to interact with directly.

And I thought about Paul too. His situation and his loneliness. How he could have been a supported and contributing part of the community around him if someone had just given him the tools he needed in order to make that happen. The ideas and plans I would need to create A Bright Future, Inc. started coming together in my mind even then.

But I still had some lessons to learn before I could transition into that CEO. And one of those lessons was going to be extremely difficult.

Soon after that fateful day at the tutoring center, I returned home to something I had hoped to avoid but I'd also come to expect: an eviction notice on our apartment door. As hard as both Michelle and I had worked (she worked while she was pregnant but stopped working after our daughter was born), it still wasn't enough to pay our rent on time and in full. At that point, we needed to get creative about how to deal with the fact we would have to move out—with a baby who we needed to find a way to shelter and provide for. The rest of that story, though, is for the next chapter.

Before we get into that, I want to help you see how you can also be BRAVE when it comes time to confront difficult roadblocks that have the potential to stop your goals or dreams. In the story above, I was tempted to quit. It might seem like a simple thing to keep reading when everyone is judging you, but for me, it wasn't. Mindset scarcity came in hard. And mindset scarcity is an issue that will pop up in your life too.

At this point in my story, I was definitely seeing some wins. I met Michelle. We had our daughter. I passed the CBEST. But scarcity was still hanging around with its familiar presence. It came through resources—our lack of income as Michelle stayed home to take care of our daughter while I had to find multiple jobs. It came through emotions—the challenges I faced as colleagues told me students wouldn't be able to understand me well because of my thick accent.

And I fell short. We were evicted from our apartment. But I didn't give up, dear reader. And you can keep going too. As long as you know how to leverage scarcity by being BRAVE. That's what we're going to cover next.

The BRAVE Framework

When you find yourself in a moment where scarcity wants to make you stop, like I did in reading that text aloud, there is a way you can reframe the difficulties you face—the roadblocks—by turning up your creativity. In my case, it often meant reaching out to the people in my life and using an external opportunity to overcome the adversity, but that isn't the only option you have. Let's take a look at the different moments in the BRAVE framework and how they will help you use creativity to overcome whatever roadblock you face.

How to be BRAVE:

1. **B**reak down the barrier.
2. **R**eframe the scarcity.
3. **A**dapt with your available resources.
4. **V**isualize new paths.
5. **E**xecute boldly and endure.

Now, let's take a deeper look into what each piece of the framework will help us do.

Break Down the Barrier

When you see an obstacle, instead of thinking about it as something you won't be able to get past, you can break it down into its different parts. So, ask yourself, *Exactly what is this problem made out of? If I break down this obstacle by looking at the things that contribute to it, can I set myself up to be less intimidated?*

When you encounter a roadblock, instead of stopping, you can figure out how to get around it. And then, once you've done that one time, you have started to collect methods for getting around the different roadblocks you encounter in life. That is how you leverage mindset scarcity: Take what seems huge in your mind and break it apart so that you can deal with manageable chunks of adversity one at a time.

Reframe the Scarcity

Once you've noticed the kind of scarcity you're up against, whether that's emotional, mindset, or resource scarcity, you can reframe it, which is exactly what I'm talking about whenever I encourage you to leverage scarcity.

When you look at scarcity as an invader, you are going to try to avoid it. But by looking at it as a companion (one you've seen visit me again and again in my life), you can think of it as either an internal or external opportunity. In my case, the difficulties I experienced pushed me outside of my comfort zone in different ways until I figured out exactly what kind of educational support person I wanted to become (which you'll see more about in the next chapter).

Without the external opportunity of needing to make money, which forced me to be open to so many different places and ways of teaching, I wouldn't have been able to found A Bright Future, Inc. At the same time, internally, I was proving to myself how brave I could really be. This was a huge opportunity for me because it allowed me to show up consistently each day knowing I could make it through whatever happened.

In this chapter alone, you see how mindset scarcity gave me a gift by presenting an internal opportunity. By directly confronting the fear of having to speak with my accent in front of many students and parents and getting through that challenge, I was able to give myself a confidence boost that I carried with me throughout my teaching career.

And you can see how through resource scarcity—needing a better-paying job as a husband and father—I was able to realize an external opportunity through the relationship my wife's aunt had with the principal of the school where I had led the after-school program.

So, how can *you* reframe the roadblocks scarcity brings into your life so that you can leverage that scarcity?

Stop, look, and leap.

Stop means take a mental pause. Even if that means you only take 30 seconds to determine what the scarcity issue is. When I was teaching in the classroom reading that prompt aloud, I didn't have a long time to acknowledge the problem I faced. But I took a few seconds to observe what was happening so that I had time for the next step: look.

Look is what you do after you've paused. You notice what is going on. You weigh your options. And you acknowledge the type of scarcity that you need to leverage in that specific situation. Once you've thoroughly looked at it (which doesn't have to take a lot of time, like you saw with my situation in the classroom), that's when you can plan how to take the next step: leap.

When you *leap*, it is because you have looked scarcity in the face, determined which internal and external opportunities you have available to you, and then take bold but imperfect action. You don't have to make sure your leap is perfect, but you do need to leap. Leaping can be as simple as reading aloud when people are staring due to your accent. Because being BRAVE means taking action to respond to what is happening around you. So how do you do that when life gives you unexpected gifts in the form of scarcity? Let's take a look inside the next step of the BRAVE framework.

Adapt With Your Available Resources

A lot of people think that they need x, y, and z in order to adapt successfully to whatever is going on around them. But that's not true. You can look at what you have in terms of the people and things around you to adapt to the character of scarcity showing up in your life. (Which we're definitely going to see a lot more of in the next chapter.) If you look at what kind of scarcity you're facing, that's where you can find the opportunities within the roadblock you're experiencing.

While I definitely encountered resource scarcity in this part of my story, I was able to work multiple jobs, build new skills, and leverage the relationships I had to pivot and adapt as I leapt from opportunity to opportunity to make sure that I was providing for my family, all while going after my goals and dreams. I didn't let the roadblocks keep me from focusing on my vision.

And you can also adapt to the roadblocks you face as long as you are willing to use the resources available to you *right now*. That means you leap before you think your situation has become ideal or perfect.

Next time you come up against a roadblock, visualize all of the different ways that you can get around it. And don't stop at just one approach. Visualize every single solution you can think of.

Adapting is key to moving forward, but you also need another tool to help you leverage the kind of mindset scarcity that roadblocks can bring into your life. It's time to visualize.

Visualize New Paths

Creative solutions or opportunities present themselves when we are willing to visualize different routes around the roadblocks we encounter instead of just trying to force ourselves to use what seems to be the most obvious opportunity we have.

Even though Michelle and I were struggling financially, we were still willing to dream together about being able to rent our dream house someday. We dared to believe that those dreams were possible, even if that meant I had to go from job to job as I worked to increase my level of education so that I could make the kind of money that would allow our dreams to become our reality.

Eventually, as you will soon learn, I was able to make our dream come true. It just didn't look the way I thought it would.

And finally, after you have done everything else in the BRAVE framework, you can learn to execute.

Execute Boldly and Endure

As you work through any of the roadblocks that come into your life, your brain will scream for you to stop. That's exactly what happened to me when I was in that classroom feeling self-conscious about my accent. But your brain will also do something else when you encounter scarcity-induced roadblocks: It will stall. This happens because your brain sees multiple things going on and wants a clear answer to how all of these things will fit together—even when that answer isn't available. This leads to overthinking which can prevent you from taking action.

So instead of getting caught in a trap where you overthink everything you could do or everything that could happen, I want to encourage you to execute a decision—do *something*. And when you experience discomfort because your brain really wants you to wait, to stall, then endure that discomfort. You will get through it. But you won't make any progress if you allow your mind to keep you from moving forward. And there's another important reason why you should choose action. Let's find out what it is.

Why should you take action even when your brain is screaming for you to stop?

Because when you act, you allow the creativity associated with you figuring out what to do next to be exercised in a way that allows your creativity to grow. And that is always a good thing. That's when the creativity you used to solve the roadblock in the first place will multiply and help you. In your life, you will make an exponential number of decisions—some that your brain will want to keep you from making. But you will need to push through that temptation to stall as you work toward your goals and dreams to live out your vision.

So when you execute boldly (decide how to act and take action) and then endure the discomfort that follows (usually because your brain wants to wait to gather more information before acting), that is when you start to make real progress as you work through one goal at a time. This is how you leverage mindset scarcity.

And now that you know how to be BRAVE, let's take this opportunity for you to practice using the framework.

Reset, Restart, Repeat

As you think about the different roadblocks you've faced in life, there is an opportunity to adjust your future approaches by using the BRAVE framework. You can come up with a creative solution to your scarcity-related problems by using five BRAVE questions.

1. What exactly is the roadblock I'm facing, and if I break it into parts, which piece can I work on first?

2. How can I reframe the scarcity (whether it's resource, emotional, or mindset scarcity) into an internal or external opportunity for growth?

3. What resources, skills, or relationships do I already have that give me access to help in the situation I'm facing right now?

4. What are five possible paths forward and which one makes sense to take today as I act boldly?

5. Once I take that first step, how will I encourage myself to endure the discomfort related to refusing to let my brain stall me from taking action, and how can I repeat this process tomorrow?

Now that you know what these five BRAVE questions are, think about a roadblock you are currently facing as you work to complete one goal that will bring you closer to living your vision. Then, go through the questions again to see what creative answers you can find so that you can work through that particular roadblock.

CHAPTER 8
The Battle for *When*

Every life is full of movement. Quick moves. Strong moves. Weak moves. Short moves. And each move is affected by one thing: momentum. Sometimes I would make a move that helped me glide along for a while. Other times, as hard as I would try to create momentum, the movements would be short and quick. It was those short, quick movements that didn't really take me where I wanted to go that reminded me how close scarcity can stay—day in and day out—and how friction can slow my momentum. And while I didn't always face these struggles knowing exactly what to do, by this point in my life, as a married man with two children to provide for (one in the US and another back in Côte d'Ivoire), I had learned that no matter what happened, I needed to maximize whatever momentum I had.

We all face different seasons of *when* in each of our lives: moments when difficulties and possibilities clash together and we have to fight for another chance at trying again. This was a time when I had to keep every ball rolling around me as

I worked toward the goals I had brought over from Africa to America with me.

You see, all different types of scarcity will create friction in our lives. Scarcity wants us to slow down, to stop. In physics, if an object is at rest, it will stay at rest. And if it is in motion, it will stay in motion unless another force comes into the picture to slow it down. This is exactly what friction does. And when we're thinking about how scarcity can act in our lives, sometimes it becomes a point of friction.

In order to leverage scarcity instead of letting it halt our momentum, we have to keep going with whatever we have. Even when friction comes in to slow us down.

When we finished the last chapter, you saw something happen to me that caused a lot of friction—and therefore a lot of scarcity—to enter my life: My wife and I, along with our baby daughter, were evicted from our apartment.

As it turned out, substitute teaching hadn't brought in enough money to pay our bills, even though I had created a plan for our lives that I thought would work. And something far more difficult had also entered our lives: Michelle's delayed grief as she finally started to work through the loss of her own mother. So, as we take a look at this next season of my life—where scarcity was once again a primary character—I want you to remember what I was trying to hold onto: momentum.

Healing for Me, Delayed Grief for Her

Earlier, when I shared with you about the numbness and the scarcity of grief I faced when I lost my mother, I told you that having my son and seeing my mother's smile on his face had healed a large part of my heart. What I didn't realize was how much my daughter would heal the rest of it.

When my daughter was born, I looked at her face and saw a miracle: I saw my mother. This time, the child had more than just my mother's smile. All of her features were touched by my mother's features. The moment I saw her, my entire heart filled to bursting with joy. But my wife didn't have the same emotions I did.

She experienced what I would call delayed grief. Experiencing motherhood for the first time compounded the grief she felt from really never knowing her mom, who had died when Michelle was very young. This specific brand of the scarcity of grief was stronger than I ever could have imagined. And it brought Michelle to a difficult season of *when*—a time that would shape the future of our relationship. While I didn't have words for what she went through back then, today I suspect medical professionals would call it postpartum depression.

As I watched her suffer, I tried to keep whatever momentum I had. Despite our eviction and eventual downsizing to a one-bedroom apartment, I worked more and more hours, and that only drove Michelle's depression down deeper and deeper. Looking back, I wish I had been more of a resource to her as she battled emotional and mindset scarcity. But I didn't know what I didn't know.

And as our daughter grew and Michelle slipped further into isolation, an external opportunity was offered to me that I couldn't refuse.

The Internship

After working in the Richmond School District as a substitute teacher, I learned that one of the speech therapists, Dr. Pauline, was heading up a new program that focused on helping teachers gain their special education teaching credentials while they worked in different schools that needed these types of specialists. She encouraged me to apply, and I got in. This paid internship program was offered through Sonoma State University and would allow me to gain important teaching experience while working toward my teaching credential. While I studied and prepared for whatever was coming next, I couldn't imagine the place I would end up at for my final year of the internship, where I was required to teach and would be evaluated.

This is what my learning schedule for the internship looked like:

For the first two years, I worked and studied nonstop to pass all the tests that would allow me to get through level 1 of the internship program. That earned me my official teaching credential.

The third year repeated the same schedule, but I was working toward my level 2 test. If I passed that, I would be able to enter year four where I would be a student teacher. Once I got through that, I would be eligible to go for my master's, which I knew would significantly improve my pay and my ability to take better care of my family—both Michelle and our baby girl, and my son back in Côte d'Ivoire.

So I worked hard. At the same time, I experienced resource and emotional scarcity. We didn't have a lot of money even though I was being paid to study as part of the internship, and Michelle was suffering in a way that meant all she could do was take care of our daughter. She was no longer able to give me inspirational speeches or dream of the future with me. Just surviving each new day as a mother while confronting her own delayed grief wore her out completely. As I took a survey of what my reality looked like, I realized I needed to fight against scarcity—against friction—to keep whatever momentum I had.

If I stopped moving forward, even if I had only been making progress an inch at a time, I knew I would stop everything completely. My dreams would cease. The visions of who I could become that I had while looking across the bridge in my youth would die. And that's also when I came up against one of the biggest challenges of my life: my internship assignment.

Their Last Chance at Again

For my teaching assignment as part of my special education program, I was given the task of teaching 11 special needs students who had been placed in that particular school as an alternative to juvenile detention. The time they had with me was their last chance at making something out of themselves. And another intern had been placed in the classroom next to mine with the same number of students; these young men were also part of what I would call the "last chance" program.

But the number of students I was responsible for changed quickly when my fellow intern quit. The students were too much for him to handle.

So the program directors presented me with an external opportunity—one I didn't even consider saying no to. They offered me the other intern's class, along with his pay. This meant I would have to work harder (and invest longer hours into preparation for twice as many students), but my pay would be more, and I would be able to save money toward graduate school.

I understood graduate school was the only way I could maximize the amount of money I would be able to make. So, I said yes. Working with these 22 young men was going to be my primary focus during this particular season of *when* in my life. I kept going to school and working to support Michelle and our daughter, but these young men needed another *again*, and this was the *when* that allowed me to give that to them.

I quickly realized, though, that one of the reasons my fellow intern had quit was because the age difference between the interns and the students didn't give us enough of a gap to allow the students to see that we were qualified to work with them. That we were people who were older that they should try to listen to.

Imagine, I was only 28 at the time, and these students were between 18 and 22. And 90% of them had criminal backgrounds from selling drugs to committing armed robberies and shootings. Many of them had been part of different gangs. With this reality, I thought about that old character, scarcity.

I was facing resource and mindset scarcity in that I didn't have the life experience I needed to deal with kids with these backgrounds, and I didn't know how to encourage myself each day to believe that I could actually get through to them.

At the same time, I felt personally responsible for their success because my class was their last chance, and I didn't want any of them to end up in jail.

It was my job to help them deal with specific learning disabilities or learning difficulties that were related to autism or trauma. My goal was to educate them in English, math, science, and history as well as help them modify their behaviors so that they could reintegrate back into the general population (back out in their respective communities as contributing young men).

And while I didn't know *how* exactly I was going to do all of those things, I did know there was a *who* that could help me. Let me explain.

Becoming Coach Carter

You already know that I had lived and worked in Richmond, California. But what I didn't tell you was that the principal I worked for as a substitute teacher was the same principal that the famous Coach Carter had worked under.

So, when I thought about who could help me reach these boys, I thought back to the movie *Coach Carter*, starring Samuel L. Jackson, that had been released in 2005. The real coach, Ken Carter, had worked at Richmond, and had been able to impact inner-city boys from that area with his strict methods. He demanded that the players maintain a certain grade point average (GPA) because he wanted to see them go to college on basketball scholarships, and when the boys let their grades drop, he locked the gym until the kids could bring their GPAs up.

Coach Carter used difficult exercises to teach the players discipline, including pushups and suicides. If you're not familiar, a suicide is grueling drill where you start on the baseline of the court, then sprint and touch the ground on the free-throw line and return to the baseline. Next you sprint to halfcourt and return to the baseline, then again to the further free-throw line and return, and finally the opposite baseline and then all the way back to your side's baseline again. This is no easy task. In the movie you watch as the players have sweat dripping down their faces from their hearts pumping as they prayed for that last suicide run.

I decided to study the methods depicted in the movie and created my own Carteresque personality to wear when I was with the young men. Obviously, I couldn't have them do pushups and suicides, but I could use Samuel L Jackson's Coach Carter mannerisms to prove to the students that I was serious. I needed to seem older and wiser than I was. With Coach Carter in mind, I created a persona that still honored my goals but that gave the students a reason to respect me—to listen to me. Because if they wouldn't listen to what I was trying to teach them, then I couldn't help them.

In working with the students with physical disabilities, especially the ones who were in wheelchairs, I thought of my mother. Of how I had wanted to serve her after she had experienced her stroke. In helping these students, I saw it as the same as helping her, which was an important *why* for me as I went through this season of *when*.

So there were two things I was responsible for—and at the same time. On one hand, I had their academic portion of learning where I had to cover English, math, science, and history. Then, on the other hand, there was the emotional and behavioral component, given their criminal backgrounds. I had to help them acknowledge and work through aggressive and self-injurious behaviors (SIBs) and get their occurrences reduced while helping them test at their grade level. All to reintegrate into the general population outside of the school once they graduated from this second-chance program.

At the same time, I was also able to help many of my students reconcile with their families, which was huge for them.

The *When* Starts to Crumble

I poured everything I had into helping these young men. All of my emotional resources went to them, which meant there was basically nothing left for me to invest at home and in Michelle in her season of intense struggle. She was isolated with our daughter. And I wasn't there for her, which was my failing as a husband. This is where the *when* of separation came into my life.

Michelle said she needed a break. I told her that I wanted to take care of our daughter, and she agreed to shared custody so that she could have visitation when she wanted. So, in essence, I suddenly became a single father. In the next chapter, I'm going to share what that transition was like. But for now, what you need to know is that I was taking on too much, and it was about to catch up with me in some very real ways.

Aside from my marriage, working at the school with these second-chance students brought up another uncomfortable feeling. When the students graduated from the program, I couldn't help them anymore. I knew they still needed services, and sending them into the world without continued support felt horrible.

That feeling of discomfort further fueled my desire to create a service where I could help foster kids who had aged out of the system. I was also concerned for adults with learning or physical disabilities who still needed help past what the education system could provide after they graduated from high school. The seeds of my company, A Bright Future, Inc. were being planted firmly in the ground during this *when*.

But like I said at the beginning of this chapter, one of the ways that scarcity gets into our lives is through friction—it tries to stop us from moving forward with momentum. And even though so many things were starting to fall apart in my *when*, I knew that I had to keep going. Yes, I was about to face some of the most intense scarcity of my life, but if I stopped, my dreams were dead—and I couldn't let that happen. Too many people were depending on me.

In this moment, I want you to know that you don't have to let your dreams die. You can keep moving with the momentum you've built despite the friction you experience (which you're going to read more about in a minute). In my story, you can see that a lot of the momentum I harnessed came at intense times of friction: after my accident, during my internship, and while I was gathering the seeds of what would grow into A Bright Future, Inc.

But before we get more into harnessing momentum when there's friction, I think it's time to reflect on what we've gone through so far.

First, you learned how to look at the opportunities around you—both internal and external. Remember, the opportunities around you will help you leverage the different types of scarcity.

Then, you discovered how to create tools out of the scarcity you face and to use trial-and-error approaches to learn from failure as you figure out what you will need and how to find access to those things.

Next, you found out how to build a dream so that you could focus on a specific vision for your life and set up goals to allow you to live out that mission.

In chapter 4, we talked about the ASK framework, which helps each one of us understand how to ask for help (even when that isn't our first instinct).

After that, in chapter 5, we walked through the RISE framework, which helps us discover how to work through the unique scarcity of grief. Because it is inevitable that we will all face loss in this life. But that doesn't mean we can't keep building dreams and pursuing our visions.

In chapter 6, you learned the steps to be able to leverage flexibility through the FLEX framework—so that you can work through even the most difficult moments of scarcity.

Finally, in chapter 7, you discovered how to face difficulties with a courageous outlook by using the BRAVE framework. Being BRAVE means that you can break down problems to find solutions as you continue to pursue your mission, even when your brain wants you to shift to an easier path.

As we close out this chapter, I want to help you see that you can keep whatever momentum you have too. Yes, even in the face of each of the three different types of scarcity.

How? It's time to learn about the MOVE framework.

How to MOVE Forward

Even though scarcity enters our lives through friction, either to slow us down or to try to stop us, we can still continue to move forward.

That doesn't mean keeping the momentum you have will be easy, but with the MOVE framework, you can decide the best way to keep going forward, no matter what type of scarcity is there or how much of it you face.

The MOVE framework will guide you through taking continual steps:

1. **Measure** the movement.
2. **Own** the friction.
3. **Visualize** the victory.
4. **Engage** the *who*.

So how does each one of these steps work to keep you moving? Let's break each one down as we think about emotional scarcity, resource scarcity, and mindset scarcity.

Measure the Movement

Earlier I said that some of the movements I would make were smooth and would help me glide. Other times, the movements were short and quick. To help you recognize *when* you are moving and how that movement is happening, let's take a look at the different ways you can leverage each type of scarcity to measure the movement. That way you'll be able to adjust your moves forward.

The first step, measure the movement, is the most important, so we're going to spend a bit more time unpacking this one than we will with the other three steps.

When you face **resource** scarcity, that means you are running out of *something* that will help you continue to move forward. The friction is getting to be too much. But, you don't have to stop measuring your movement forward just because you lack resources. By now, you know that throughout my life, I have lacked many different resources at different times. But I was able to move through these times of scarcity by celebrating every resource win—not just the big ones.

For example, I used to have to find bus fare to get to and from my home when I went to that fancy high school back in Côte d'Ivoire. On the morning ride in, I would thank God for that trip. And once I found the support I needed from a friendly uncle near the school, I could get home. And I thanked God for the bus ride back.

But what does it look like when what we lack isn't a resource but a supportive feeling?

When you experience emotional scarcity, even small emotional shifts are wins. Did you express your emotions in a healthy way? That's a win. Did you overcome something difficult and discover strength you didn't know you had? Yes—acknowledge that. This is how you keep momentum, even in emotional scarcity like grief. When I lost my mother, I felt so stuck I had to leave—to get away from reminders of my deep, tragic loss. That was how I kept moving forward.

Mindset scarcity shows up as hopelessness—it threatens to stop you from within. Friction can come from your own thoughts. Think back: How many times have you felt hopeless? Now ask, how many times did you choose hope over despair? You're still here. You're still you. That means you've made measurable movement, even in the midst of mindset scarcity.

In the next chapter, you are going to read about my separation and what it was like to become a single parent. I have to tell you, there were moments when I felt like I didn't know what I was doing. That I had lost something precious to me even though my actions had caused that loss. That was a huge season of mindset scarcity for me. But I had my daughter. I had my students.

And I knew I had to keep going—to keep *moving* forward. And you can do the same. Acknowledge the mindset scarcity you're experiencing. Name it. From there, you get to decide how to act. How to hope. How to keep moving forward.

Be sure to measure that movement to prove to yourself that the friction of scarcity isn't going to keep you stuck in any one place. Next, let's take a look at what it means to take ownership of the friction that threatens to stall your momentum.

Own the Friction

I shared with you before that scarcity wants to slow us down. Friction enters our lives to stop us. But we don't have to let it. And the way we fight against this slowing down is to own whatever scarcity brings into our lives. No matter which type of scarcity we need to own.

Owning resource scarcity starts by identifying what's lacking—time, money, space, or energy (beyond a cold brew with fancy foam). When you name what's missing, you can get curious about how to fill the gap and find creative ways to keep moving—like I did after the ambulance accident, when I had to relearn how to speak and walk.

With emotional scarcity, curiosity about what you're feeling—and why—is key. Are you numb, like I was after losing my mother? Angry? Overwhelmed? Too tired to care? Naming the emotion helps you uncover solutions and gives you permission to move forward. Ignoring feelings creates friction. Finally, in mindset scarcity, ask what you're telling yourself. Are you cheering yourself on or stuck in self-pity? My students in the second-chance program lost momentum when they doubted themselves—but when they borrowed my belief, their mindset shifted, and so did their movement forward.

And you, dear reader, can borrow my belief in you as well. I believe that you are totally and completely capable of keeping the momentum you create so that friction doesn't stop you. So that scarcity doesn't get in your way. You can live the life you've dreamed of. You will live that life.

That brings us to the next step in the MOVE framework: It's time to visualize your success.

Visualize the Victory

You know what it was like for me growing up. I needed to go to the bridge where I would dream my seemingly impossible dreams. Because I was able to visualize them, they ended up becoming my reality. But scarcity, as it will do, threatened to halt my dreams by introducing friction into my life—and I didn't want to let that happen.

Scarcity will work to cloud your vision, but you don't have to let it. You can visualize what you want to bring it back into focus so that you keep your momentum forward. Let's look at how.

When resource scarcity creates friction, use your imagination to picture a future where the limitations are behind you. What you lack doesn't define you, but what you dream and do shape who you become. And looking to your vision can help when you don't feel like maintaining momentum. I used this approach often while living in the US, discouraged but driven by the image of my son's face back in Côte d'Ivoire. He needed me to keep going, to make our sacrifice count by realizing my dream of becoming a CEO.

You can also imagine your way through emotional scarcity—a moment of peace, a step toward healing, a reconnection with someone you love. Then, when mindset scarcity appears, picture yourself grounded in truth, not fear. Ask, *What does momentum look like right now?* Movement will shift as life changes, but each step counts. Visualizing your progress will help you celebrate what's possible and fuels a stronger, more hopeful mindset.

Now, let's look at the last step of MOVE, a concept you have seen throughout the book but that is worth mentioning again.

Engage the *Who*

In every moment of scarcity I have faced, I always thought about finding a *who* that could help. Even when that *who* was a group of ants.

One of the ways that the friction of scarcity can interfere with our momentum is by trying to isolate us from the supportive friends and family that surround us. In my story, you saw that when I first moved to the US, I would go sit in public places just so I could talk to someone—*anyone*. I knew that if I stayed in isolation, I wouldn't be able to keep moving forward. There are three questions that you can ask yourself when you feel like friction is coming into your life through isolation. And each one corresponds to one of the three types of scarcity.

To address resource scarcity ask yourself: *Who has the access to insight about the things I don't have, that I need, who might share?*

Think back on the ASK framework and the lessons you've learned about creating a support system and looking for people who will encourage you along your way. You do not have to go through life alone. When you get curious about who can help you, you're leveraging external opportunities—opportunities that come from things outside of yourself. The key to maintaining and growing your forward momentum in the face of resource scarcity is engaging the *who*. Now, let's move to the next question.

To address emotional scarcity ask yourself: *Who has the strength of encouragement or the softness of empathy that I need right now?*

Isolation takes your emotional energy while fellowship builds it. So when you are struggling to keep forward momentum in the face of emotional scarcity, it's time to reach out to someone who can help. Even if all that person does is validate the feelings you're experiencing, that is enough to kill the friction that threatens to stall your movement. Don't try to do life alone because that will only make emotional scarcity more intense, and you won't be able to leverage it.

To address mindset scarcity ask yourself: *Who believes in me when I forget how to believe in myself?*

We all need people who will cheer for us when we're struggling: those helpful individuals who will remind us of all we are when we feel lost. Next time you find your mindset has been telling you that you *can't*, engage with a *who* that will remind you that you *can*.

To help you practice your MOVEments, let's do an exercise together.

Reset, Restart, Repeat

Journal through the following questions to show yourself how you've been able to MOVE forward already. This will allow you to set the right expectations for your mind by showing it that you can absolutely keep moving forward with momentum because you've already done it in the past.

1. What forward motion have I made in the last week? It could be physically, emotionally, or mentally.

2. As I think about the most difficult type of scarcity I experienced in the last month, can I name exactly what it was and identify if it was emotional, resource, or mindset scarcity without judging myself?

3. What has momentum looked like for me in the past when I encountered scarcity and didn't yet know how to leverage it?

4. Who has helped me believe in myself in the past? What did they say to remind me of who I am?

And if you need help with weekly check-ins, you can use the prompts below to finish the statements.

The MOVE Through Scarcity Check-In

Measure

One way I moved this week was…

The type of scarcity I was facing was…

Own

The friction I'm feeling now is…
I think it's caused by a scarcity of…

Visualize
My vision for this season is to…
When I experience victory, it will *feel*…

Engage
Someone who inspires me right now is…
A small action I'll take to stay connected is…

CHAPTER 9

Isolation Again

There are moments in every journey when what you were pursuing becomes a thing of the past. Your priorities change. As I've seen many times, life happens to and for you and confronts you with truths that cause you to ask, *What is it that I really want out of my time on this planet?* As I entered yet another season of isolation in my life, this was the question I faced.

In this chapter, you are going to see some huge moments that happened to me. The more I think about my life, the more I can trace the way my vision was about to change to one thing: the loss of my mother.

Now, you've read about the group home boys, the children with learning and physical disabilities, and the young men who were in a last-chance situation—and how they were all a huge part of my story.

And you've also read about how each time I would work with someone who needed my help, especially someone who was in a wheelchair, I would think about taking care of them as if it were another opportunity to care for my mother. Doing those things for her, on her behalf, in small acts each day to help heal my grief subtly shifted my goals.

At this point, I realized I no longer wanted to be a wealthy man being driven around by a chauffeur, like the influential people I had watched back in my youth as I visited the bridge where I dreamed. I now wanted to make a difference for the young people I saw struggling in a system of schooling and "justice" that wasn't ever really created with them in mind.

Yes, I still wanted to make money. I needed to for my son and my daughter. But money alone wasn't enough to satisfy the passion that had been growing inside of me all along: the intense desire to help.

The fire that had been growing inside of me for so long had such intense heat that it was about to survive some of the coldest, loneliest moments of my life. Even more lonely than when I had spent my days talking to the ants.

As we travel through this extremely trying part of my story, notice that even though I was failing—in so many ways—it was my passion to help others that moved my life forward. Because you can use your passion to do the same—but only if you are determined to make your light shine bright.

Now, it's time to revisit a season of a new kind of isolation in my life: a trying time when I hit yet another crossroad where I could choose who I wanted to be. This starts with a house full of promise that became a potential black hole.

The House Trap

As I've shared, I wanted to be able to help the boys and young men I worked with at the school, but there wasn't a way for me to offer them ongoing services. Some of my friends in the special education space told me that I should consider going into support and independent living services, so I started to create a plan.

One of the biggest pieces of my new plan was to purchase a large house that I could eventually turn into an adult group home. That way, I could make my dream of taking care of others the way I wished I could have taken care of my mother come true. I had a good job, as I was still getting paid to teach two classes at the second-chance school where I wore my Coach Carter–inspired personality. So when I went to get a loan to buy the house, they told me I could afford to borrow up to $700,000! But I didn't understand how that could possibly be the case.

I had really only wanted to borrow $300,000. At that point, Michelle and I were separated. I was raising our daughter on my own because I had asked Michelle for shared custody, and Michelle allowed our daughter to live with me. After all, my daughter looked like my mother, and I loved her so much—I couldn't imagine not being the one to take care of her. Plus, in the midst of all this, I was studying to get my level 2 teaching credential and master's degree from California State University, Sacramento.

When the agent told me to take out $700,000, I couldn't imagine paying the mortgage for that along with my tuition and supporting my daughter. So, I agreed to take $575,000 for a large house I found that I felt would be the perfect group home someday.

Then the housing bubble in the United States popped and all the house prices plummeted. It was 2008. Looking back, like so many other people experienced in those days in the US, I realize that the bank lied to me. They said I could afford things I just couldn't afford.

Almost overnight, the house I had a $575,000 loan on was only worth $150,000. Around that same time, I was going through a divorce. Michelle and I had decided to stop being a married couple, though we would stay best friends and work together as co-parents. With the way everything happened, I suddenly found myself without enough money to pay the mortgage.

Scarcity was back. But by now I knew what to do: I needed to leverage the resources I did have. One of which was time. I mean, as a single dad who worked two jobs, I didn't have a ton of it. But I did have more time than money.

I had heard that because of the crisis, it was possible to get a loan modification. You see, the US had bailed out Bank of America (that was who I had my loan through) to keep them from failing to help people like me in this really difficult situation. But Bank of America had tried to keep the bailout money for itself. It wasn't until homeowners in California filed a class action lawsuit that the banks would start to allow for loan modifications.[6] And even then, it was an uphill battle.

---

6   "California Homeowners File Class Action Suit against Bank of America for Withholding TARP Funds," National Mortgage Professional, April 8, 2010, https://nationalmortgageprofessional.com/news/27379/california-homeowners-file-class-action-suit-against-bank-america-withholding-tarp-funds.

Since I was in a city with a corporate Bank of America headquarters building, that's where I went. Not to a local branch, but to the main office. When I first met with a representative there, they told me, "Well, we're not going to modify your loan."

Based on what I had learned about the situation of reduced home values from housing nonprofits in my area, I couldn't make sense of what the banker was telling me. While Bank of America tried to discourage me, thanks to the various counselors who spoke with me, I knew what my rights were—especially in light of the bailout. So, I said to the banker, "What you don't understand is I am going to fight you guys all the way until the end." Because of the help I had gotten from local groups who were advocating for homeowners during this time, I knew that if I missed two payments, that would be okay, but if I missed three—that was when they would foreclose. That meant I had three months to figure out a solution to the house-trap puzzle I was in.

So many times in my life, as I went through resource and emotional scarcity, I had felt totally isolated. But I knew that I needed help. That's why I sought out advocates in local nonprofits who could give me more information, even though they didn't have all the answers either. Still, I knew I would not survive this next wave of potential destruction in my life if I stayed in isolation.

It was 2010 by this point and my divorce with Michelle was close to being finalized.

My dream for turning the home I had purchased into a group home seemed like it was never going to happen.

Before I tell you what did happen with my house, I want to share how I was able to go through a divorce without letting the potential for scarcity there destroy the friendship that Michelle and I still had.

The Most Important Question

When Michelle first asked for a separation, a few of the people around me said that I was in for one of the biggest battles of my life. Even with some of the people in our church, the divorces they had gone through had turned ugly—fast. But I knew that wasn't what I wanted for Michelle and me. We had shared so many beautiful moments together, and she had given us our daughter.

Even though I didn't necessarily want a divorce, I understood that I hadn't given Michelle enough emotional support during her delayed grief, the most difficult time in her life. I had chosen my work over her too many times. So I wanted to release her from the marriage if that was what she wanted.

That's why I didn't feel the need to hire a divorce attorney. And she didn't either. I asked her the one question I knew would help us both move forward in a way that would allow us to maintain our friendship: "What do you want?"

Michelle was extremely fair with what she asked from me. She could have tried to get more. So I looked at the amount she wanted, broke it up into payments I thought I could afford over the next few years, and we finalized our divorce agreement through arbitration instead of having to go before a judge.

She agreed to joint custody of our daughter, who we agreed would live with me. That's when I became a single father. Thankfully, the terms of our divorce meant Michelle still felt comfortable around me, and she remained a part of both my daughter's and my lives. I know that our divorce story isn't typical, but I also know that if more people were determined to look at all the reasons they had to be thankful for what some would call a "failed marriage," then a lot more families would be able to move forward in a healthy way like we were able to.

Don't get me wrong, the season of isolation that followed was difficult. All three types of scarcity surrounded me. I didn't have much emotional support. My resources were dwindling, and I was facing foreclosure. And my mindset was something I had to work hard to preserve each and every day—at work at each of my two (sometimes three) jobs, at school, and those few sweet hours when I was home.

A big, immediate need I had was to find daycare for my daughter that was near her school. But I needed a place where she could stay the night when I worked too late to be able to pick her up. I spent so many hours helping people, but once again I found myself without a big support system. Thankfully, the woman who ran the daycare where I eventually enrolled my daughter became like a sister to me. She supported my daughter when I was working, which then supported me because I knew my daughter was being well loved, even when I was at work.

I can't tell you how I prayed, trusting that God would help me make sense of everything I was going through. That He would turn my difficult circumstances into something good. I knew that God saw how much I was doing to help the young men at the second-chance school. That I was dedicating my life to helping others by getting a level 2 credential and simultaneously beginning to build programs for adults who needed independent support and other services at one of my part-time jobs.

It wasn't until the class action lawsuit against Bank of America was decided, though, that my prayers were answered.

A Moment of Relief

In the background, with everything else going on, I had still been randomly going by the Bank of America headquarters to ask repeatedly for a loan modification. After the class action lawsuit was decided, someone from the bank called and said, "What you wanted us to do, we're going to do, and even more. We're going to reduce your loan to what the house is now worth—$150,000. That means your mortgage payment each month will go from $2,500 to just $900." The good news meant I could still pursue my dream of helping others that was inspired by the loss of my mother, even if I wasn't going to use the house as a group home.

This was yet another moment in my life when I recognized that it was vital for me to keep trying as long as the situation still existed. As the saying goes, it's not over until the fat lady sings. But what I want to tell you—that most people won't—

is that there are so many moments when the fat lady is still getting ready. She has to drive to the venue. She has to prepare mentally for her set, get dressed, and put on her makeup. She has to warm up and rehearse. Until she is on that stage, singing that first note, there is still time—so don't give up.

When it came to my mortgage situation in the burst bubble of the housing market, I could have done what most people were tempted to do: used the money I needed for the mortgage payments to go on vacation while they foreclosed on my home. But instead, I talked to advocate after advocate. I learned what the law said based on the bailout money the government had provided. And I filed every form required so that if they happened to consider giving me a loan modification, they had everything they needed. So when the judge told Bank of America that they had to use the funds the government had given them to create loan modifications, my name was on a list of people who had done *everything* already. That's when they called with the news I needed so badly.

Yes, I was able to keep my house. But my ideas about using it as a group home had already begun to change because I had faced the potential reality that the house might be taken away. Even that scary thought ended up being a gift, as it sparked the idea that would become my business, A Bright Future, Inc.

And as we close this chapter, I want to help you see that you still have plenty of moments where you can interrupt the fat lady before she sings—but only if the passion you have for what you want to do with your life lights a bright fire inside of you.

Your Response to a Great Need

In this chapter, I talked about a huge shift that happened in my mindset. Growing up, I used scarcity as motivation—I didn't want it to control my life or my children's. I had fought for things as small as bus fare and didn't want that for them. After losing my mother and working with young people with disabilities, I began to see my mother in each person I helped. The desire to care for others the way I couldn't care for her became my true passion. For a long time, I carried that passion alone, unsure how to use my skills and lacking the resources to build a team—at least not yet.

What I will show you in the next chapter is that there was a huge need for someone to solve the problem I was passionate about solving—and that meant people would pay me to realize my passion!

And that is the kind of passion you need to have so that you can live a life where *you* leverage scarcity like I did. Here's how it works.

Turn Your Passion Into Your Professional Purpose

Step 1: Identify what you are passionate about doing in the world.

Step 2: Realize a need that people have (one they will pay you to solve) that you can meet as you live out that passion.

Step 3: Create a system inside a business you work for or that you start so that you can get paid to solve that problem.

Step 4: Become the owner of that business (if you didn't found it as an owner) so that you can control your own destiny as you work to help others.

We all need money, which is why creating income is part of this process. However, money will never motivate any of us long-term like fulfilling our passion and living out a mission and a vision will. And now, as I'm writing this book in my fiftieth year on this planet, I can see that money alone would have never motivated me like my purpose and passion to help others. Just like money can't motivate us long term, leveraging scarcity solely for our own personal benefits isn't enough of a reason to keep going either. Especially when things feel hard (or in this chapter, for me, downright impossible). But having a passion to help others—whatever that looks like for you—is what will take you really far.

It's passion that challenges us to leverage scarcity even when we lack the emotional support, resources, or mindset to move ourselves forward. It is by thinking of and caring for others that we can truly succeed. As we move into the next chapter, using my own life as an example, I am going to prove to you just how true this is.

First, though, let's walk you through an exercise where you can identify what your passion is. So that you can ignite the fire and burn bright in the arena of your choosing—as you focus on solving a problem for the people who need your help most.

Reset, Restart, Repeat

In this exercise, you will work through different prompts to uncover your deeper motivation for helping others so that you can transform it into a mission that meets a real need in the world around you.

Make sure to grab a notebook or write notes in your phone based on your answers as you work through the four steps that will help you turn your passion into your professional purpose.

Give yourself plenty of time to think about and write answers for each prompt. This is an exercise you won't want to rush through.

From Scarcity to Significance

Step 1: Identify what you are passionate about doing in the world.

It's time to find *your* fire by responding to this prompt:

> Think about your past for inspiration. Identify one moment in your life when you wished someone was there to help you, a loved one, or a friend. Or when there was something that you knew you wanted to be able to help others with someday. What was missing? How did that missing piece make you feel?

Step 2: Realize a need that people have (one they will pay you to solve) that you can meet as you live out that passion.

Now, you're looking for a pattern that's already existed in your life that you can use to help others while getting paid for that help. Ignite the fire you found in the last step by responding to this prompt:

Who are you naturally drawn to want to help? What kind of problems do you feel compelled to solve—even if someone *wasn't* paying you to solve that problem? Make a list and write down as many things as you can. Resist the urge to edit it as you go and jot down every single thing you can think of.

Step 3: Create a system inside a business you work for or that you start so that you can get paid to solve that problem.

In this step, you're going to think not just about *who* needs your help but *how* you can help them—based on the skills you've built by living your life so far. Then, it's time to look at our third prompt:

Who out there needs help based on the same things that you've overcome (or helped someone close to you overcome)? Which group of people (time to think bigger) are facing the same challenges you once faced (or watched someone you care about face)? Would they pay for someone to help with this?

Now, think about *how* you would help them. What method or system can you create so that you can give each person or group the same consistent help each time you work with them? Could it be a service, a product, a program, or even a role in a company that already works to address the problem you want to serve?

Step 4: Become the owner of that business (if you didn't found it) so that you can control your own destiny as you work to help others.

Buying or founding a business doesn't happen overnight. But you can start to make a plan of what it would look like to do this in the future. Here's the prompt for our final step.

Create a pep talk that you can give yourself as you identify where scarcity is a character in your life as you work toward creating systems that support your passion. And also as you find areas where you need to build better resources so that you can be in control of how you work to turn your passion into purpose as you step into each new day. You can model it after the one I have here:

> I am passionate about helping [the who] with [the what] because I believe that the world would be a better place if [the why]. I want to create [the how] to serve them and build a life of purpose for myself.

Here's an example based on my own passion and purpose:

> I am passionate about helping young adults with physical or learning disabilities escape isolation with support services because I believe that the world would be a better place if everyone in our society had the ability to live independently and be part of a community. I want to create ways to teach these young adults how to function well in society to serve them and build a life of purpose for myself.

And now that you've done all that hard work, it's time to reflect on what you've discovered.

Reflection Minutes

Before we move on, take a few minutes and sit with what you've written. How does it feel to see past your past, your passion, and your potential all on the same page? Think about how these ideas, all combined in this way, can support you and ignite the fire of purpose that can be lit and grown based on your passion.

PART 3

START OVER AGAIN TO WIN

CHAPTER 10

Daring to Hope Again

Throughout my life, I have heard a lot of people say that the struggles that we face will make us stronger—but I think that's an incomplete thought. Enduring struggles alone won't help us grow stronger, braver, or smarter. Looking for ways to grow *through* adversity *during* struggles is what will really transform us.

I would define adversity as another form of that ever-existing character in my life: scarcity (one that by now you probably recognize as a familiar character in yours as well). Adversity and scarcity are like twins who look the same but have slightly different personalities. Adversity brings chaos that can be caused by different things into your life while scarcity brings lack.

Adversity can be defined as difficulties or misfortunes that come into your life consistently. The things I'd been experiencing up until this point were difficult. I had experienced misfortunes. But I also was determined to find opportunities in my circumstances that allowed me to dare to hope again so that I could start over again with whichever opportunity I had that could be my friend. Yes, I could acknowledge the character of scarcity in my life, but I could also find ways to start again—and win.

In this chapter, you're going to experience what I would refer to as the turnaround. Where hope finally became a constant visitor—even in the face of scarcity and in spite of adversity.

There was one man who stood out as a beacon of possibility for me, and his main word was *hope*. This man came into my life in a season where I needed to be reawakened to the idea of hope. I'm talking about the 44th president of the United States: Barack Obama.

Can I Really Hope Again?

My new life wasn't one I had planned for. I was a single dad working two to three jobs at a time while trying to make some kind of plan for what I could do with the education I had worked so hard to achieve. Thankfully, I graduated from California State University, Sacramento with a forever credential as a special education teacher, and I knew that would allow me to get a job that paid well.

But I had also spent *so* much time working, and I knew that I couldn't allow what was meant to be only a season in my life (putting in extra hours of both study and work) to take over the rest of it.

Honestly, after all of the stress I had gone through because of the financial crisis, having to fight to keep my house, and going through a divorce, I was in a state of depression. Too many things had happened around the same time, and I had difficulty leveraging scarcity successfully like I had before. While I was doing okay when it came to resources, the emotional and mindset scarcity I faced hit me hard.

I would describe myself during that time as being in a sort of functional depression. The circumstances I had been through slowly wore me down over the course of several years. What I really needed was someone to model for me what it looked like to keep going even when there was little hope. Enter Barack Obama.

I knew that to work through my emotional and mindset scarcity, I needed to invest more time into my relationship with God. And I wanted to invest more time into my relationship with my daughter. Then, one night, I was flipping through the TV channels, and I saw Senator Obama giving a speech. I was mesmerized not just by his words but by his manner—his way of being.

Intrigued, I continued to watch Obama's campaign and saw how he always took the high road and talked about hope. His enthusiasm combined with his calm demeanor captivated me. So, I started to model my responses to what life was throwing at me after the way Obama dealt with what the campaign trail was throwing at him.

I remember at one point, Obama was talking to a journalist on a television interview, and the journalist asked him something like, "You know, you're running against Hillary Clinton in the primaries. That's a big opponent. Why do you think that you can beat her?"

Obama responded calmly with confidence in every word. "Well, let's wait and see what happens on Tuesday."

His approach was to move forward and see what would happen. That made me think. *This guy,* I realized, *is a man of color like me. And he is willing to try to keep going in a world that seems against him. I can be like that too.*

And on that following Tuesday in the primary, Barack won. He beat everyone, including Hillary. He still had a long way to go before he would get elected as president, but he gave me hope. Knowing that someone like Obama was out there fighting for every opportunity gave me a breath of fresh air—and the will to keep going.

Little did I know that I was on the cusp of my dreams coming true. No, not the dream of having a chauffeur (which I still don't have, even as a CEO) and being rich, but of being able to help the people I was trained to help who also reminded me of my mother.

So I started to ask myself, *Through this time of crisis in your personal life, what hope can you see and build on, Max?*

I realized that I could see faith. Once I decided to focus more on my relationship with God, I also realized that I didn't just have hope—I had faith. I could trust God to help me navigate the scarcity and adversity I faced. In retrospect, I looked back at my story up until that point and saw how God had always provided a way through for me and my family.

With God guiding my way, I was finally ready to dream again—and to dream bigger than I ever had before. It was time to embrace a different direction, and it was one that would eventually pull me out of teaching.

The Spaces Between the Gaps

Since I had received my special education teaching credential from the internship program I was a part of, I was working with the young men at the second-chance high school during the day. But, as I have touched on, I had started working in the support-services industry in the evening. It was important to me to create some kind of system that would help the students I worked with during the day live life *after* they graduated from high school. Each evening, my second job brought me to clients outside of the school through another organization. These were clients who needed support. When I was there, I could see the spaces that needed to be acknowledged. That led me to become a special education program creator.

I wanted to fill the spaces between the gaps to help young adults with learning disabilities and physical handicaps live more independent lives. But not many organizations were focused on creating training programs for these specific individuals, so I used my education and experience to fill in those spaces. And I created a program that would allow me to train others to do the same.

However, there was another surprise waiting for me around the corner. And this time, while scarcity took someone important from me yet again, and adversity showed up to bring me new challenges, God gave me a gift that I still treasure intensely, even now.

Saying Goodbye and Saying Hello

In 2010, I lost another person who I was extremely close to: a woman from church. She had been a friend and an encouragement to me—and a testimony to our faith as I went through one of the most difficult times in my life. When she passed away, I could feel scarcity pulling at me again—always again. But this time, it wasn't just scarcity and adversity that came into my life.

When my friend was dying, she had asked me to take care of her son after she was gone. When she finally passed, her son had already turned 18, so there wasn't any way for me to adopt him legally. But I did treat him as my son in every other way possible.

He moved in with me, and we enjoyed being family for each other. The relationship we had was unique in the fact that as I said hello to him as my son, and he said hello to me as his father, we both said goodbye to his mother. And somehow, that healed whatever small pains of grief I had left from losing my mother. After all the tears I cried when I lost my friend, and the joy I felt in my heart from having another son in my life, I finally felt whole again.

It was during this second intense season of grief that I was finally able to look at a picture of my mother for the first time since she had died. It had taken 19 years for me to be able to look at her beautiful face—one I missed so much—again.

These days, I still refer to this wonderful young man as my adopted son, and I'm proud to say that he—as an American citizen—moved to my home country of Côte d'Ivoire. While he had no direct connection to the place or the culture, he experienced my stories of growing up there, and as a Black man himself, he wanted to see what it would be like to live there himself. Now, he has built a community of his own to live with—to support while he is also supported.

It was through these two unexpected events—discovering Obama and becoming a kind of adoptive father—that I was able to break out of my functional depression because I was willing to say to myself, "What hope can you see and build on?" Now, let's take a look at what asking this same question can do in your life.

The Hope You Build

Through each chapter of my story (and this book), you've seen me go from high highs to low lows and everything in between. But one thing I needed to constantly do for myself when I faced scarcity or adversity was to find a way to build hope in myself. Hope for my future. Hope for what I could do to make the world a better place. Hope for my children as their father. And hope for my changing dreams as I realized money was never going to be enough to motivate me to reach my full potential. Or to help me leverage the different types of scarcity I faced.

So how can you build hope when it doesn't come to you easily? And how can you fight to use hope as a tool to leverage scarcity, and even adversity, when the ever-present character of scarcity shows up yet again in your life? Let's find out.

Just getting through the adversity we face in life isn't enough to help us become better, stronger, and more determined to do good or to help others. However, you can use each difficult moment when you encounter scarcity and adversity to help you build your hope muscles—if you're willing to self-reflect.

When we ask ourselves, "What hope can I see and build on—right here and now?" even in the most unfortunate circumstances, we can reflect deeply on what we're going through to understand what lessons are within that experience we can learn from.

Hope isn't just a feeling: It's a practice and a discipline. This means you can cultivate having hope as a skill that can be carried into every arena of your life. Plus, a wonderful thing about hope is its potential to multiply.

The same dear friend who was ill and dying gave me hope by encouraging me, even in her extremely difficult circumstances. She had hope for going to heaven and for her son and me to live as a family after she was gone. Barack Obama had hope that even as someone who was more unknown than some of the people he campaigned against, he could create an outcome that surprised his biggest critics—even within his own political party.

Hope spreads. It inspires. And it is so much more than wishful thinking. Hope is tangible in those moments when things feel extremely hard. Through my personal journey, hope has helped me pull myself out of the different pits of hardship and desperation that scarcity has tried—and failed—to pull me into. Hope is a rope that can pull you from one place to the next. And hope has the potential to multiply and spread from one person to others at any moment.

But finding hope doesn't happen by accident. It takes purposeful thinking, doing, and being. Saying, "I can grow and build my hope muscle," is a promise you must make to yourself. It is only when we have hope that we can truly leverage all the kinds of scarcity we've touched on in these pages: emotional, resource, mindset, and grief.

Before we get into the next chapter and the collective lessons scarcity taught me about pursuing my goals, I want to encourage you to allow hope to become more than a word to you. Let it be a muscle you build and a promise you make to yourself. That no matter what scarcity tries to take from you, you will keep looking for hope to multiply for yourself and for others.

Reset, Restart, Repeat

In this exercise, I am going to show you one of the most valuable tools I have used through each phase of my life: learning how to use hope as a filter to find ways to assess and leverage scarcity. And there are two big steps you can take to do the same.

Step 1: Acknowledge the *ways* that scarcity wants to shrink your dreams.

As a single father, scarcity tried to shrink my dreams of what I could do for my children—all three of them. But when I looked at the ways scarcity tried to do that, I learned that I could counter those forces with hope. Hope that I could improve the lives of my children simply by being with them whenever possible, providing for them, and being open about how much I love them.

To practice acknowledging how scarcity wants to shrink your dreams, think back to one of the goals you identified earlier in the book or choose a new goal. Then, ask yourself the following:

How is it that scarcity is trying to shrink this goal? What is scarcity trying to take away from me when I think about how I can take steps forward to make this goal into my reality?

Now that you've identified how scarcity is trying to shrink the things you want for yourself, it's time to move to the next step.

Step 2: Look at the specific way scarcity wants to shrink your opportunities and observe where you can build more hope.

When I noticed the spaces between the cracks in the lives of the young men I was working with at the second-chance high school, I could have said, "That's just the life they've been given. There's nothing that any of us can do about it." But accepting the problem without building hope that there was a better way wasn't going to help these men. I needed to find hope to move forward to create a better solution for the scarcity and adversity they faced. And you can do the same thing for yourself.

Instead of embracing negative thoughts like, *Why is this happening to me?* or *When will this finally end?* I want you to think through the questions below and come up with answers that address the results you got from answering the questions in step 1.

How will hope allow me to shift my perspective so that I can see all of the possibilities that are possible in these specific circumstances? And what lessons has either emotional, resource, or mindset scarcity brought into my life that will help me achieve these goals?

Now, take a moment to reflect on what your answers were in each of the two steps and ask yourself, *What kind of future can I see more clearly now that I've taken time to exercise my hope muscle around the scarcity I'm facing as well as the goal I want to achieve?*

Amazing work. You are building hope as a muscle, and that is an amazing way to learn to leverage any kind of scarcity.

CHAPTER 11

Scarcity Takes a Break & the Voice of Hope Steps In

When you work hard to leverage scarcity while it remains a steady character in your life, there will come a moment when that character finally takes a break. Not forever, and not entirely, but long enough to let you feel more hope. And a hope that is beyond the muscles you've already built.

And this is the point in my story where that shift, that moment, *finally* happened.

When scarcity decides to give you a break, there is often a clear voice that transition speaks in, telling you to go, to stay, to push harder, or to rethink your approach. During this season, as I took a closer look at my life and decided what specifically I wanted to hope to do for me, that voice was there, guiding my next moves.

There came a moment in my teaching career when I realized I had reached the peak of what I could do with the degrees and credentials I had. In order to progress any further, I would either need to apply for assistant principal jobs or I would need to go back to school to become a principal. Neither of those jobs appealed to me, though. I knew that I wanted to be more hands-on with special education students specifically. And during that time, I also had another important revelation.

When I reflected on my story as a young student, and I looked at the special education students I was working with, I thought, *If I were a student today, with my physical disabilities, I would have been placed into a special education program myself.* If I had special support available to me throughout school, I wouldn't have had to try so hard each and every minute to make a way forward for little Max. A Max that had to pretend he *wasn't* deaf in one ear or that he *could* tell the difference between the right and left sides of his body.

It was the voice of transition that pointed this out to me. And you too can listen for this voice. It's a call into a different season of life—to bring your dreams, even the ones that have been transformed over time, back into your memory. I was doing the work for others that no one had done for *me.* Was it really any wonder that I was less interested in becoming a school administrator than working directly with special education students?

I prayed and asked God to direct me. I thought about my daughter and my two sons and what owning a profitable business would allow me to do for them. And I retraced every step I had taken through life, with scarcity as my welcome (and sometimes unwelcome) companion. I thought about how I could help the people I was providing services to be able to leverage scarcity for themselves.

So, with a heavy heart—because I didn't want to leave my second-chance students—but a plan for my own future purpose, I decided to start my own company with the curriculum I had been developing for independent and support services. All with the eventual goal of leaving my teaching job at the second-chance school. This would allow me to focus on my vision of serving young adults who needed help with behavioral management, better integration into their communities, and the deeper sense of "normalcy" they wanted but wouldn't have without the programs I was developing.

That's when A Bright Future, Inc. started to take off. But I couldn't complete my mission alone. I needed to challenge the resource scarcity I was experiencing when it came to adding people into my organization. But before I could do that, I had to be the all-in-one guy. The CEO and the janitor. The HR department and the payroll supervisor. And as I thought about how I could possibly manage all these roles, I kept thinking back to the hope I had found in a man—one I spoke about in the last chapter.

Obama CEO

After I met Barack Obama on the TV that fateful afternoon, watching him respond to that journalist, I realized I could look at what he was doing—the way he displayed his character and the choices he made—the same way I had looked at the way people were succeeding back in my younger school days. The same techniques and mindset would help me become a better leader. I used the characteristics and strategies he modeled and made a template for myself. One I could use as I stepped into the multiple roles I was taking on at A Bright Future, Inc.—that is before I had enough training material or financial resources to hire any team members.

The things I learned from Obama and the way I was able to create my own CEO education based on what I saw him do could fill its own entire book (which is actually my plan, so watch out for that book to hit the shelves in the future). So I won't go into them in detail here. What I will say is that Obama continued to give me hope and guidance as I stepped into a role that I had always dreamed of but didn't have any formal education in how to perform: Max the CEO.

The dreams I had back on the bridge as I watched important men drive past in their designer suits and fancy cars were coming to life, just not in the way I thought. And it was because I recognized that I was doing for others what no one had done for me growing up. So I was willing to leverage scarcity yet again, as I took on the role of everything-man inside my company. Because I was determined to continually make the world a better place.

However, that doesn't mean everything was smooth sailing.

The Voice of Warning

When I started to work with students, I could see my mother in them. And it was through my experiences with her that I developed a passion for helping others. But that was also a huge downfall of mine when I became a CEO. You see, I was determined to provide the best care, even to the most difficult clients, at my own expense. That was *my* choice, and I was the one who was directly affected.

For a while, that was okay. My first hire was a man named Doug who really understood the different service models that were available. He helped me adjust our program based on four important factors: safety, freedom, integration, and individualized care. Doug also helped me see that I needed to better shape my organizational structure since I couldn't really be the everything-man as we grew. After making some adjustments, I could finally shift the accounting, HR, caregiving, and behaviorist roles to other, extremely capable people I found and hired.

Once I had team members, and I was asking them to sacrifice themselves for difficult clients, that became a problem. I was making that choice for *them*, not just *myself*—and often, I was thinking about my mother and choosing to side with the clients over my employees over and over again.

That's when I began to receive complaints through the federal Department of Labor (DOL) —notices that I wasn't complying with what my employees expected as far as their well-being. My team wanted to feel supported and respected in their work—especially when clients were disrespectful or physically aggressive. And I had two choices at that point.

I could listen to the voice of warning (that happened to be coming from the federal DOL at this point), or I could keep going and alienate some of my employees. But without my team, I couldn't help as many people. I would be limited to myself. That wasn't what I wanted. I decided to look for an external opportunity (something I could benefit from that was outside of myself) that could help me leverage my mindset scarcity better. It wasn't working for me to look at every client as if they were my mother if it resulted in me neglecting my employees. I needed outside help to reframe my thoughts around the business and the processes I was using.

So, I hired an organizational coach.

My coach helped me transform my mindset and create a personal philosophy and company culture that was rooted in dignity, appreciation, and teamwork. He guided me to build incentives for myself and my employees that helped us change the culture, and the bar of excellence he set was extremely high.

During that process, I also realized I needed to step away from teaching. My company required more than full-time hours at that point, and I was completely burned out. I needed to leverage the scarcity of resources I had by making sure I was investing my time well. While I loved working at the second-chance high school, I knew that I was making a huge difference in my community by providing services for the young people who needed them *after* they graduated from high school.

Everything, both in the company and inside my team, was finally running smoothly. But I guess scarcity decided that I had gone on without it being a bigger presence in my life for a bit too long. Because then COVID happened.

Essential Workers and the Voice of Sacrifice

By the time the phrase "essential workers" came into being, I had gone from having a handful of team members to being responsible for over 300 employees. And we were also responsible for hundreds of clients.

Everyone in our organization was an essential worker because of the kinds of services we provided. Suddenly, I was responsible for making sure not only that every one of my team members was safe but also that we didn't bring COVID with us into any of the places where our clients were—including group homes, which became dangerous places during the pandemic.

I had to make sure that my team was fitted properly in personal protective equipment (PPE), which was difficult to put on correctly. Plus, that equipment was difficult to even get my hands on at all.

And then there was the threat I created for my kids. My first son had moved from Côte d'Ivoire to California to live with me when he was 16 before the pandemic happened. My adopted son was still living with me. And my daughter also lived with me during the beginning of the pandemic. But I couldn't risk getting them sick, so I quarantined myself in my room whenever I was home. Emotional scarcity was back as I lived in a sort of isolated trauma, scared that at any moment I could spread the dangerous virus to those I worked with on my team, those I served in different places, or those I loved at home.

Honestly, it felt like that trauma state lasted well past the time we could stop worrying about wearing PPE. Only now as I'm writing this book several years after the pandemic, do I feel like I've somewhat recovered from what that was like to live through—day after day, for months that felt like years.

During that time, I knew I had to keep going because the voice of sacrifice was asking me to—for my team and for the people we provided services for.

Throughout that entire intense season, I never did get COVID. I suspect that I got it before we knew what it was, as I was visiting New York City just before the lockdowns started. There had been a lot of visitors from Asian countries around me in all of the tourist places we visited, like Times Square. I did experience some kind of virus directly following that visit, although I can't be sure it was COVID.

As I managed through what were admittedly some of the most difficult circumstances I have ever faced, I realized yet again that life is short. And while I still work as the CEO of A Bright Future, Inc., I also began to invest my time in things that filled me up and that helped me build my hope muscle even stronger. But I'll get to those adventures in the final chapter. First, I want to help you see that even though scarcity had given me a break, it came back stronger than ever, but this time I was still able to see the opportunities it held for me—both external and internal.

New Scarcity, New Opportunities, and the Voice of Transition

When we choose to leverage scarcity instead of feeling consumed by the limitations it brings into our lives, something surprising happens: We can begin to notice the voice of transition earlier than we otherwise would. But how? And why?

Instead of scarcity happening *to* us, if we look for it early and adjust as soon as we see it, we can make scarcity happen *for* us by acting to leverage it. If we feel like something in our life has shifted, we can ask ourselves, *What type of scarcity is showing up right now, and how do I adjust my course to allow me to leverage that type of scarcity better?* This is where you can listen for that voice of transition.

As a new moment of scarcity comes into your life—whether it's resource, emotional, mindset, or grief—it always brings new opportunities with it. Let's take a look at the moments I described in this chapter and break down the events I experienced into both internal and external opportunities that leveraging scarcity allowed me to see.

The Internal

Because of what I was going through internally, I was able to do the following:

- Realize that, as a student today, I would have been in special education; this clarified my drive to help others like me.

- Choose to build needed support services instead of following the traditional school leadership path.

- Learn to balance care for clients and employees, treating everyone with the dignity I wished for my mother.

- Face burnout during COVID and recognize it as mindset scarcity, relying on past experiences to manage the pressure.

- Take advantage of external opportunities available during that season.

In that season, there were also external opportunities I had access to.

The External

By looking at the external opportunities in front of me, I learned to do the following:

- Model my leadership and CEO journey after Obama's words and actions.
- Hire Doug, whose experience reshaped our client-service approach.
- Work with an organizational coach who helped me build a stronger, more supportive team culture.
- See that COVID brought stress but clarified my priorities: protect my team, refine systems, focus on service, and make time for joy and family.

During every new phase of transition, I could look for and find both internal and external opportunities that had been introduced to me through scarcity, that old friend (and sometimes enemy). With everything you've learned in this book, you can now do the same thing—in each and every transition you face. As we walk through our final exercise together, I want to show you how you can find the opportunities in scarcity during times of transition where you need those opportunities most.

Reset, Restart, Repeat

Whenever you hear the voice of transition in your life, you can take three steps to explore your two types of inventory to understand where the opportunities are.

Step 1: Your Internal Inventory

Think about the journey you've been on so far. Then answer the prompts below to look for opportunities where you can grow, become more aware of what's going on, and identify how you can further build your hope muscle.

1. Make a list of all the internal resources you have right now: your mindset, skills, family relationships, etc.

2. When you hear the voice of transition, survey the different types of scarcity you're facing. What resources do you lack? What emotional experiences do you need? What mindset can you have to make progress?

3. How can you use what you've learned so far in life to build a process around that transition to help you keep moving forward?

4. What would you say your new, focused goal is in the midst of this transition?

Step 2: Your External Inventory

Now, you'll look at the opportunities that scarcity is bringing you from outside of yourself—the external ones. Answer these prompts to complete this second step.

1. Make a list of all the external resources you have right now: the relationships outside of your family, the products or equipment, the intellectual resources, etc.

2. What calling do you have in life that is associated with the transition you're in? Is there an external person who could help you understand this transition better? Or a resource or program that would help?

3. If your transition is also bringing you some sort of crisis (like what I experienced with COVID), is there anything you can use from what someone else has given or taught you in the past to help you?

Step 3: Connect the Dots Between the Two

Now that you know what your internal and external opportunities are, you can look at the different answers to the prompts you came up with and see how they complement each other. Answer this final round of prompts to make those connections.

1. What patterns can you identify between your internal and external opportunities? Do any of them fit together in a way that will help you leverage scarcity faster?

2. Think about how you've leveraged scarcity in the past. What can you do right now, as you face the transition you're in, to create impact or meaning for yourself and the people you care about or are responsible for?

3. What is the next internal decision or external resource you need to embrace as you continue to move forward?

Feel free to use this exercise as many times as you need to as you listen to the voice of transition whenever it comes into your life.

CHAPTER 12

Arrive at the Win

When you've been acknowledging and leveraging scarcity for decades, sometimes you start to lose hope. You get tired of always having to look at which internal and external opportunities you have. It can feel almost impossible to leverage mindset scarcity as you start over again and again. But at some point, if you don't give up, you are finally going to arrive at a win—where you are able to realize one of your goals. And that is where this chapter brings us: not to the end of my story, but to the arrival of a win. Several wins, actually.

While I was writing this book, I turned 50. And that many years' worth of lessons have taught me everything you've read in these pages, and more. But one thing I want you to understand is that I wouldn't be who I am today without scarcity.

Were there moments when I wanted to scream, cry, or both when I noticed the character of scarcity appear in my life yet again? Yes. And I have cried many tears. But I have also experienced moments of intense joy. I don't think, dear reader, that you can experience one without the other. The presence of scarcity and having to leverage it made each joy I have experienced sweeter and more meaningful.

What will it look like for you to experience those moments of joy? What opportunities is scarcity constantly bringing into your life? And how will it feel when you finally win? To help you get some ideas of what arriving at the win might look like in your life, allow me to tell you about the wins I found in my life—alongside scarcity.

The Professional Win

Creating and running my own company, A Bright Future, Inc., has completely changed my life. Now, I am privileged to lead a team of people with compassionate hearts who provide hands-on, individualized support for vulnerable individuals so that these individuals can thrive in whatever environment they're in.

I still think about Paul, that young man who was completely alone at the first group home I worked in—what a gift of awareness that he gave me. He taught me what my professional passion was. Paul gave me an opportunity to keep the promise I made to myself to take care of my mother—even after she was gone. Because of my mother and Paul, I was able to build something that is a force for good in my small corner of the world, Northern California.

At A Bright Future, Inc., our mission has grown as we learned and created programs to help each individual person we serve to live a healthy and productive life in their own community.

The mission we have mirrors the deep belief I've developed through my story—the one I've shared in these chapters. Every day, it is our goal to help our clients find stability and heal from trauma or neglect as we provide coordinated care for them. We walk with them and their families toward lives that are marked by dignity, independence, and purpose.

At the same time, I have been able to provide financially for my family and be more present with them as I learned how to ASK for more help, to RISE when I encounter the scarcity of grief, to FLEX when I go through something new, and to be BRAVE when I face moments in my life that feel intimidating or even impossible. Once I had all of those abilities, I was able to MOVE.

Everything I learned from the most intense moments of scarcity I could have imagined taught me how to keep going for all of the Pauls in the world that I want to help and do good for. Now, I get to support and lead an amazing team who multiplies the amount of good we can do as an organization.

This is a *huge* win. But it's not the only win I've experienced as a result of learning to leverage scarcity.

Family Wins

While I have worked hard to make sure that my kids didn't have the same extreme encounters with scarcity that I did, they are still facing their own challenges as they live their lives, and I am so proud of them.

At the time of writing this, my daughter is in college in Southern California. She ended up moving in with her mom when she was around 16, and I am so thankful for the relationship that my daughter and Michelle have.

Michelle and I are still the best of friends and support each other as co-parents.

My son moved from Côte d'Ivoire to live with me in Northern California when he was 16 and studied in university to become an accountant. He will graduate with a degree soon, perhaps even before this book is officially published. While it was so difficult to be away from him in his younger years, the relationship we have today is so important to me, and I am thankful for every moment we've had together.

And my adopted son moved from Northern California to my home country of Côte d'Ivoire to build a community made of uncles, aunties, friends, and family to live the kind of life he wanted. He is also an extremely talented musician.

I am a blessed father and love being there for my kids and also helping them realize their goals as they move into different phases of life. These are my family wins.

And I have also recently learned something new that I want to share with my kids: how to balance our lives well by pursuing even more moments of joy through extra activities that I call passion projects.

My Passion-Project Wins

After COVID, I realized that I needed some outlets for my creativity that were more about experiencing joy. Since I have an amazingly capable and well-trusted team at A Bright Future,

Inc., I can now devote time to two things that I'm passionate about: real estate and entertainment.

First, I learned how to invest and manage real estate in a different state—Illinois. This challenge has allowed me to do everything from make plans to work with my hands in an extremely satisfying way. I learn something new about the industry each time I work on one of the projects—and more importantly, I learn new things about myself and what I'm capable of.

I've also been able to create a production company that works with younger artists to create shows, films, and—my favorite—music. In a few weeks, I'll even be traveling to London to support some of the artists my brand represents as they perform live. Toward the beginning of my story, I shared with you how influential French television and music was in my life and the lives of my siblings. And now, I get to be part of the creation process that goes along with the specific kind of joy that comes from entertainment.

Now that you've seen my wins and how they continue to show up in my life, it's time to focus on what *your* wins can look and feel like.

Your Wins

When you started this book, you were beginning a new journey—one where instead of avoiding scarcity (which is impossible to get away from in this life), you learned how to leverage it. I hope that along the way, you have seen how scarcity, as a character in your story, has also presented numerous internal and external opportunities. And the best part is, even as scarcity continues to show up as you travel forward in time, you know how to greet it with open arms as a friend—one that will keep teaching you how to learn and grow throughout your entire life.

And as you start to have your own wins, I want to encourage you to stop and reflect on all you've been through. I hope you pause for a moment and reflect on how you have been able to leverage all three types of scarcity: resource, emotional, and mindset.

By reading this book, you have put yourself in a position to do more than just to realize your dreams, like I did when I finally became the kind of CEO I envisioned all those years ago on that bridge. You've also gained the knowledge you need to surpass your dreams and turn them into a vision that can make the world a better place—especially in your own corner of it.

All those years ago, I would have never imagined that I would build a business that would have supported someone like me, my mother, or Paul. But that's the path that leveraging scarcity led me down.

So, I want to ask you one really important question as we end our time together: What epic and inspiring win will being able to leverage scarcity get you in your life?

If you can dream it, you can plan to do it—and while you're on your way to making those dreams into reality, you might just dream up something even bigger and more impactful that you can do to improve the lives of the people around you.

I believe in you, and I have hope and faith that you can leverage scarcity just like I did. You've got this. Now go out into the world and be brave. Each time you face scarcity and realize that the change you need to make is bigger than just making a simple adjustment, it's time to look at the opportunities you have to see where you could start over. Then, start over to get that win.

Parting Gifts as You Start Over to Win

As a gift for you as we finish our time together in this book, I've created a comprehensive assessment that will help you see where you can focus more specifically on leveraging scarcity in your life. Plus, I have four classes where I break down the ASK, RISE, FLEX, BRAVE, and MOVE frameworks so that you can use them with an extra layer of support. To access these gifts, please head to www.MaxKonan.com.

I want you to know, dear reader, that I appreciate the time you invested with me as you've read my story and learned how to leverage scarcity yourself. The next time you face transitions or needs as you live out your vision and your mission, think back to all of the hard-won thoughts you worked through as you learned about that ever-present character: scarcity. I believe in you, and I can't wait to hear how *you* were able to leverage scarcity in your own life.

With a heart full of gratitude,
Max Konan

ABOUT THE AUTHOR

Max Konan is the founder and CEO of A Bright Future, Inc., a mission-driven company that helps adults with special needs live independently and thrive in their communities. Born and raised in Côte d'Ivoire, Max grew up dreaming of a life that once felt far out of reach. After facing various challenges in his home country, Max immigrated to the United States and rebuilt his life from the ground up—multiple times.

Through years of personal reinvention and professional dedication, Max has transformed scarcity into strength. He has a unique passion for helping others learn with compassion and clarity. Max's work is guided by his belief that starting over isn't failure—it's the foundation for creating a life you were meant to live. His writing draws on the storytelling tradition of his West African roots, offering wisdom, encouragement, and practical tools for readers navigating setbacks, scarcity, or unrealized dreams.

Max is a devoted father, passionate mentor, and lifelong learner committed to helping others leverage their challenges to create meaningful lives. He also has a passion for entertainment, including film and music—which he harnesses as a part-time producer.

ACKNOWLEDGEMENTS

I would like to thank God Almighty for allowing me to reach the point where I can share my life experiences with His creation, you the reader.

To my wonderful children, I thank you for brightening my days and being incredible individuals.

To those who are no longer with us but were instrumental in my upbringing and my thriving to overcome the challenges I faced—you know who you are and I want to say thank you.

To my brothers and sisters for being with me during my journey.

To those who the Lord has trusted me to work with, I am honored to have met you and thank you for keeping me on my toes.

To all my colleagues, thank you for working for my companies and supporting my vision to make the world better.

To the reader, it is my greatest wish that this book will allow you to overcome whatever issue you are facing so that you can reach the transformation you seek. Reach higher. And thank you for trusting me with your time as you read through this book.